Twelve Paintings

Twelve Paintings
Tal Sterngast

Excursions in the Gemäldegalerie of the Staatliche Museen zu Berlin

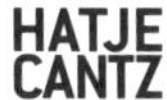

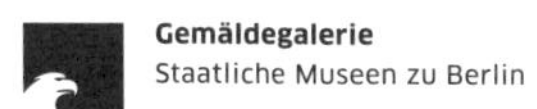

To Amalia

Preface

In her analyses of twelve outstanding works of European painting, Tal Sterngast unites the craft of art criticism with unsparing social inquiry. In her singular reading, the film scholar extends and sharpens our perspective of the works in question; for in these paintings, the products of bygone centuries, she perceives contemporary life's gravitas and volatility. Sterngast stresses not so much the archaic quality of these museal objects, but instead their current relevance and significance to both art-historical and sociopolitical reflections and insights. These are perhaps more important today than ever before. With her book, the author offers us fresh views at old works.

A moment of doubt and unease led Sterngast to visit the Gemäldegalerie in Berlin in 2016. The momentous political developments and upheavals of recent years had just begun, and their social and moral consequences—which continue to profoundly shake structures that until then had appeared stable—were no more than a shadowy foreboding. Sterngast came to the Gemäldegalerie hoping that these centuries-old works of art could provide the guidance to "return to the present, better equipped," as she writes. I am happy to report that her quest was successful, as well as remarkable. Through encounters with what was familiar, the author discovered the exceptional.

Besides the author, who happily accommodated my request that she assemble her essays on works from the Gemäldegalerie into book form, I would like to thank everyone who contributed to the production of this publication—my colleagues in the General Directorate and the Gemäldegalerie who worked on the content and editing of this book, as well as the staff at Hatje Cantz Verlag for their time and efforts.

Michael Eissenhauer
Director General of the Staatliche Museen zu Berlin
Director of the Gemäldegalerie, Skulpturensammlung
and the Museum für Byzantinische Kunst

Introduction

Tal Sterngast

The world as I thought to know it came to an end in late 2016. The result of the Brexit referendum in Great Britain in June activated my reality principle as a distortion. That year's swelteringly hot summer in Berlin clarified, too, that irreversible changes on a global scale would dictate our lives from that point on. Finally, in November, Donald Trump was elected President of the United States, complementing the sense of reality-as-nightmare. Realness lingered away from life, or rather, unrealness penetrated it so much, blurring the difference between all categories. Nevertheless, life seemed to go on.

All of this indicated a profound break in the paradigms of representation in this moment of time. A collapse informed by the dissolving of reality into "reality," but also by the transgression of what we consider human: in the interfaces between organic and inorganic, in the invasive character of social media and in variations of the "return of the repressed" (which renders shame obsolete and breeds populism), either as a symptom of a major crisis or as the crisis itself. Not unconnected to that, the fostering and acknowledgment of the inner merits of artworks seem to make more and more space for external values—political, cultural, or sociological—that now dominate almost all areas of contemporary art making, writing, and exhibiting. Suspicion and mistrust in images coincide with suppression and a redefinition of what is allowed and what is forbidden, as new sensitivities inherit the old ones. The more uncertain facts in reality become, the more vague, unfamiliar, or terrifying they and their prospects are; and the more uncertain it becomes what images are and what purpose they serve. Why are artworks still being made and exhibited? Who needs them? Who are their viewers?

At the end of that year, a feeling of being repulsed by current affairs led me to the Gemäldegalerie, a place that was brand new when I moved to Berlin in late 2000 and that still preserved a specific sense of the city, hardly detectable now in other parts of Berlin. Almost a decade after the Berlin Wall had fallen, the building, housing the reunited Berlin state collection of European paintings from the thirteenth to the eighteenth centuries completed in 1998 (planned by the Munich architects Hilmer & Sattler und Albrecht) was placed at the top of the Kulturforum's hill. This "piazzetta," a Brutalist slope of cement and granite, leads to but also separates the former West Berlin culture conglomerate from the street and passersby.

Planning for the museum complex began around 1967 and was constantly interrupted by controversies, still noticeable in the fractured ensemble. Meant to serve as an ersatz for the cultural holdings left behind the Berlin Wall in the early postwar days of Berlin, the district's architectural beacons were also meant to mark West Germany's return to the family of free nations, and no less, a defiance of the German Democratic Republic. Most prominently, it first included the New National Gallery pavilion (1968) by Mies van der Rohe, a modernist icon of steel and glass meant to house twentieth-century art.

According to Hans Scharoun's original vision of the district, the Philharmonic Hall (1963) and the State Library (1978)—both with golden metal mesh draping their facades with elaborated curved compositions—created a soft backdrop that meant to harmonize with the forested front of the adjacent Tiergarten park and to serve as a complex but pluralistic place for everyone. In contrast, Rolf Gutbrod's Brutalist layout from 1967 suggested a built landscape that exposed its own construction, in the few buildings remaining of his initial plan. The new Gemäldegalerie rejected this historical urban planning context and rather sealed itself from its surroundings.

Intentionally reminiscent of Karl Friedrich Schinkel's Altes Museum (Old Museum), the building corresponds to an aristocratic palace, with an enfilade choreographing the viewers' pace chronologically along the north-south axis in a two-kilometer sequence through seventy-two rooms, colored velvet coverings for the walls, and paintings arranged in a salon-like hang. A large empty hall bisects its center, representing the Alpine frontier in a spatial gesture, one of several that were perhaps meant to be generous or grand but ended up being simply slightly odd. To me, the Gemäldegalerie seemed as worldly as it was local, pretentious as it was humble. Its architectural denial of recent history (with its wounds and scars) and its very surroundings created an island that remains, in a way, like the collection itself, not organic in its environment, and preserving palpable artifice.

If the present seemed to move toward such an unprecedented brink of change, what did it still share with the older worlds that this collection represents? While the corpus of knowledge and discourse regarding contemporary art seemed to reference almost only the near past, Old Masters were mostly left to forensic scientists and art historians. Perhaps restricting myself to this specific, local collection for a while would offer some latitude. One by one, I chose twelve works hanging in the galleries, already carrying a certain patina, as objects of observation in order to return to the present, better equipped. The essays, each dedicated to one painting, were first published in the weekend supplement of the German newspaper *Die Tageszeitung*, on a roughly monthly basis, starting in November 2017.

In the breadth of this selection, painting can be seen as it discovers itself along dichotomic coordinates—the optical and the tactile, the geometric and the organic, illusionistic and spiritual, religious and atheist—and becomes a medium through which modern subjectivity formulates itself. Each painting in focus unfolds its own emergence and concrete pursuits as they also reflect, presumably, something of today's concerns. Two temporal and spatial (geopolitical) axes cross my selection: first the east-west axis, divided by the Mediterranean Sea, where routes lead from the ancient to the modern world and from Greco-Roman to Christian hegemonies, from Orient to Occident; and second, the art-historical north-south axis, with the southern Renaissance at its core radiating from Italy to beyond the Alps.

Every painter, Gilles Deleuze wrote in *Francis Bacon: The Logic of Sensation* (1981), needs to recapitulate the history of painting, and thus each writer may recapitulate painters' recapitulations. I approached the paintings like the contemporary art I have been writing about for the past fifteen years. I wanted to treat them as an art critic would. That is why the fields of ideas surrounding the artists and their work are considered, and the essays jump from high to low resolution, from bold generalizations to very specific details. The choice was guided by my current concerns and tastes. It does not necessarily reflect the emphases of the Berlin state collection.

When the general director of the State Museums of Berlin, Michael Eissenhauer, suggested that we collect these essays in a book, it was the most generous, appealing invitation and proposal for both me as a writer and for these texts, allowing them to become more than sporadic publications in a newspaper. A text is also a space, and writing is the process of creating this space and getting lost in it at the same time. The writing is only completed by the reader, who by observing it from outside ends the writing. So, last but not least, this compilation is also a journal of sorts—of my expeditions to the Berlin gallery, but also into writing itself; to what these twelve paintings taught me about the possibilities of writing and thinking about art.

It was an honor and great challenge to allow these essays to be turned into chapters within a broader story. This would not have been possible without Ulrich Gutmair, who carefully translated the texts from English to German and edited them first for the newspaper and then for this book. The transition from articles to essays in this publication was also skillfully mastered by the book's English editor, Kimberly Bradley. I would like to express my heartfelt gratitude to both of them.

The Museum as a Safe Space

Amor Vincit Omnia (1601–02) by Caravaggio

Caravaggio's painting *Amor Vincit Omnia* still has the power to halt viewers in their tracks. The boy's hand behind his naked body directs the viewer into the painting to the figure's other side. Although the painting addresses and is provocatively committed to confronting the viewer, it also orients them toward the back of the work. The painting evokes a space that opens to an illusionistic distance, an extension of the real space of the painter in the studio, and the viewer in the gallery.

In a radical search for the roots of abstract painting, the American painter Frank Stella asserted that Caravaggio invented a new kind of pictorial space that projects itself beyond the surface of the picture plane and into the space of the beholder, engulfing and subsuming it. We find ourselves caught up within this sphere, whose effect can be compared to a gyroscope, a spinning object capable of accommodating movement and tilt.[1]

The year 2017 may be remembered as a time when art was attacked from within. That summer, *Open Casket* (2016), a painting by the American artist Dana Schutz, was exhibited as part of the Whitney Biennial in New York and caused an art-world uproar. Schutz's painting depicts an iconic image of the African American struggle for equality, namely the 1955 photograph of the lynched fourteen-year-old Mississippi boy Emmett Till, whose mutilated body was exposed in an open-casket funeral that his mother insisted upon. Critics and artists demanded that Schutz's painting be not only removed, but also physically destroyed. In the heated discussion about "Black anguish, White guilt," or who does or does not have the right to use

1 Frank Stella, *Working Space* (Cambridge, MA and London, 1986), pp. 1–22.

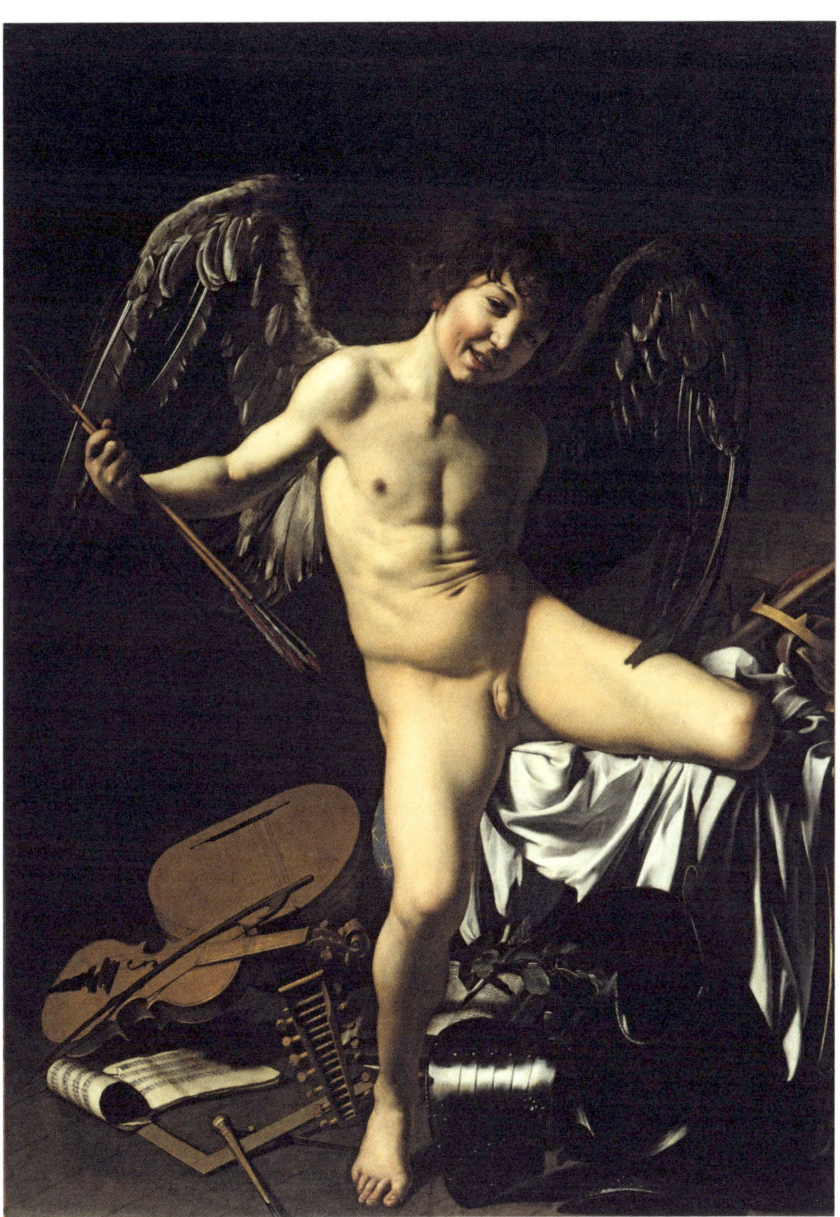

certain images in works of art, there was little debate about *what kind of painting* Schutz had made. No one seemed to be reaching beyond the intention and the work's being a cultural sign; something meant to be read and interpreted. Pictorial parameters and the ways the painting addresses its viewers seemed abolished from the general discussion. It is worth noticing that a peculiar feature of *Open Casket* that may have intentionally or unintentionally stimulated the furor was never addressed: there is a certain indifference to the subject matter, despite the artist's statements to the contrary. The work seems to have been shaped the exact same way that all Schutz's paintings were painted before or after it—as a jolly, Expressionist illustration. The painting circulated in the media, disconnected from its exhibition context—Twittered, Facebooked, and Instagrammed.

A few months later, two New York sisters in their mid-twenties launched an online petition asking the Metropolitan Museum of Art to remove or restrict the presentation of *Thérèse Dreaming* (1938) by Balthus. The subject of the painting, on view in the Metropolitan since the nineties, sits with her head turned, eyes closed, and a knee raised to expose her underwear. On the floor, a cat, a frequent motif in Balthus's paintings, drinks milk from a dish. The picture is boldly painted in warm brown tones. The pubescent model Thérèse Blanchard, who was about twelve at the time she sat as a model for Balthus, was the artist's neighbor in Paris. She appears alone, with her cat, or with her brother in a series of eleven paintings completed between 1936 and 1939. The painting is beautiful and prurient: the girl's cheek, nose, and lips are flush in reds and her arms lifted, as is her knee, in a revealing position that seems absurdly relaxed. Glowing and haptic, tactile and smooth, the exposed flesh of her hands and legs is both still and alive. Even the cat seems carved, just like the Cezanne-esque still life arranged on the wooden table behind Thérèse: glass vases, a can, and a Cubistically-depicted cloth that refers to the loose white underwear toward which our view is elegantly led—the heart of the scandal.

More than 11,000 people signed the petition, aided by a tailwind of outrage following the exposure of Harvey Weinstein's misconducts in Hollywood and the #metoo campaign. One of the petition's initiators, Mia Merill, who was an art history student at New York University, warned of the objectification and sexualization of children, which in her eyes the painting romanticizes.

Although admired by significant postwar artists (in Paris, Pablo Picasso acquired a painting from the *Thérèse* series while Balthus was still painting it), targeting Balthus was not an unexpected move. Throughout his career, the acclaimed and exceptional Polish-French painter, Balthasar Klossowski de Rola (1908–2001) was surrounded by an aura of forbidden erotic sensuality fused with an unquestionable timelessness. Over six decades the subjects of his figurative paintings remained primarily young girls, which he depicted in domestic interiors, street scenes, or landscapes blending Renaissance frescoes (Piero della Francesca and Andrea Mantegna immediately come to mind) with nineteenth-century French Realism and early Modernist figurations toward abstraction.

The new sensitivities of identity politics, lately reloaded and bluntly articulated in the art realm, have reduced both Schutz's and Balthus's paintings, and maybe painting in general, into literal pictures in which one sees an image within the circulation of media images, equivalent to an advertisement in its impact. Such reductive evaluation is remarkably questionable, if not plainly cant. More sexualization, appearances of abuse, and objectivization can be found in a Calvin Klein ad than in any given painting. Moreover, images circulating through social media, pervading every bit of our awareness today, are created by internalizing these very parameters of "objectifying," which are now utilized as both self-expression and a business strategy. This new wave is a zeitgeist powered by good grounds and reasoning that is nevertheless blind to ambivalence, thus abolishing a forceful source of interest, beauty, and gravity that has been fueling visual art for thousands of years. *Thérèse Dreaming* presents a duality within the complex relationship Balthus establishes with the painting's beholder: one in which the artist's own vulnerability is also involved, an evident identification with the seductive girl on the threshold of adulthood and clearly displayed in the painting.

In Jacques Lacan's theory of psychological development, the mirror stage is described as the moment in which the child discovers its own subjectivity—its separateness not only from the surrounding world but also from its mother. Transposed into a historical framework, according to Michael Fried,[2] Caravaggio's mirror image is a "moment" in art history in which the primordial self-enchantment of art making is confronted with self-awareness, with the artist celebrating the discovery of his detached artistic self and simultaneously expressing the traumatism this entails.

Why, then, such outrage? That artworks can incite aggression, or even violence, is historically evident, but do these incidents indicate something beyond themselves? In 1997, about twenty years prior to the New York petition and shortly after the inauguration of the new exhibition spaces for the Gemäldegalerie's painting collection in Berlin, many paintings from the collection had to be put behind glass (the exhibition architecture did not take this into consideration; today the unplanned reflections when viewing the paintings is inevitably noticeable). The protective glass was ordered because a man who had been damaging artworks with acid since the 1970s was said to have booked a hotel room in Berlin.

While the man's personal pathology may remain opaque, I would speculate that the urge to performatively damage artworks individually or collectively is inherent to the complex relationships between visual art and its viewers. And that, possessing symbolic meanings, they reoccur metamorphosed throughout history, driven by archaic powers, first theologically laden, then secularly modernized. In the late summer of 1794, Abbé Henri Grégoire, bishop of Blois, presented to the French National Convention a report about the destruction caused in the early months of the French Revolution: "A hateful distortion of revolutionary principles," he wrote. His report's title included a new term, "vandalism," which immediately became a household neologism describing systematic revolutionary violence and acts of cultural destruction against art and architecture. With negotiable historical accuracy—rooted in French chauvinism, he made an effort to distinguish between the noble Frankish tribes and the barbarian Vandals—Grégoire was referring to the sacking of

2 See Michael Fried, *The Moment of Caravaggio* (Princeton, 2010).

Rome in 455 by the East Germanic tribe of Vandals that finalized the demolition of the Roman Empire, leaving the following generations with only fragments and remnants of Roman art.

On March 10, 1914, the suffragette Mary Richardson entered the National Gallery in London and gashed Venus's back in Diego Velázquez's *Rokeby Venus* (1647) with a meat chopper, wounding the painting as if it were human flesh. She was protesting the arrest of a fellow suffragette, questioning in her act the meaning of (female) beauty. "I have tried to destroy the picture of the most beautiful woman in mythological history," she later wrote "as a protest against the Government for destroying Mrs. Pankhurst, who is the most beautiful character in modern history. Justice is an element of beauty as much as color and outline on canvas." In 1974, at the Museum of Modern Art in New York, Tony Shafrazi told the guards, "Call the curator. I am an artist," minutes after he spray-painted the words "Kill Lies All" high across Picasso's *Guernica* (1937). He later became a leading art dealer and gallerist in New York. In 1975, Rembrandt's *The Night Watch* (1642) was slashed with a bread knife by a man fighting off a museum keeper, telling bystanders he was doing it for the Lord's sake. This is just a brief list of peculiar, highly poetic incidents of art vandalism.

This specific type of aggression toward pictures is connected to the disputes over art that preoccupied the art world in 2017. In the past three years, countless further cases of canceled exhibitions, censored or Photoshopped artworks and films have shown that the tables are turning from aesthetic concerns internal to the artwork to more political concerns. The paradigms of thinking about art and its exhibition are shifting.

Amor Vincit Omnia is undoubtedly the most provocatively confrontational picture in Michelangelo Merisi da Caravaggio's oeuvre. The work's original owners, the Marquis Vincenzo Giustiniani and his brother, the Cardinal Benedetto Giustiniani, are said to have kept it behind a dark curtain, disclosing it to visitors only after certain conditions were fulfilled. The banker and the cardinal, both intellectuals, were Caravaggio's most significant patrons and two of the most advanced art collectors in the 1590s and early 1600s in Rome. Such was the circle of Caravaggio's supporters, consisting of the elite of the Roman aristocracy, banking, and high clergy; people of exquisite taste who knew to appreciate the kind of elaborated scopophilic occurrences that Caravaggio's paintings offered.

Indeed, the painting, which has been in Berlin since the Prussian King Friedrich Wilhelm III purchased it from the Giustiniani Collection in 1815 alongside five other Caravaggio paintings, of which only two survived World War II, attracted resumed attention in Berlin in 2014 with an open letter that demanded it be removed from the exhibition due to its confrontational child sexuality.

The portrait that shows Eros in sharp mirrorlike high-contrast realism glares with an unconcealed, evident seduction. As is often the case with Caravaggio's paintings, we can sense the presence of the particular model. Here, the sitter, not older than thirteen, is wearing meticulously depicted feathered wings. Despite his young age, his smile seems experienced, as does the positioning of his naked body. His left leg is folded backward in a ninety-degree straddle, while the right leg touches the floor. Smiling disparagingly and enticingly at the viewer, he seems to be enjoying himself despite the absurd, clearly unstable posture.[3] His left arm and hand reach behind him, indicating the source of pleasure he is offering the viewer. The sitter has been identified as Francesco Boneri, who probably lived with Caravaggio and may have also shared his bed. Boneri modeled for Caravaggio in subsequent paintings. Later, he would become a painter himself and to be known as Cecco del Caravaggio. The boy seems to be leaning his weight between a covered bench and a blue globe with yellow stars. On the floor and the bench several objects are masterfully rendered: a suit of armor, musical instruments, a notebook, a quill pen, a compass, and a laurel wreath.

In *Amor Vincit Omnia*'s gyroscopian composition (to follow Stella's metaphor) the orthogonals, instead of appearing to be anchored at the image's periphery and projecting themselves inward to the vanishing point, appear to project themselves outward from a central axis that coincides with the figure's penis and resumes with the points of the bow, wings, and feet. As the painting's title (in English, "love conquers all") proposes, love, or, in this case the anatomical instrument of male physical love, supersedes all dimensions adorning Eros: death (the black wings), music (musical instruments), knowledge (the notebook, quill pen, and compass) and war (armor, laurel wreath).[4] But this victory—implied in the V-shaped protractor and in the enlarged letter "V" opening the song in the notebook, as well as the name of the patron Vincenzo Giustiniani—may be just as unstable as Eros himself, leaning on the globe.

The Metropolitan Museum in New York rejected the petition for the removal of *Thérèse* and stood by its commitment to display the painting. The Whitney refused to take Dana Schutz's painting down. The Gemäldegalerie rejected the idea of hiding *Amor Vincit Omnia*. However, the demand to provide clarification to the masses or ultimately replace the picture ("They can easily hang another painting," the Merrill sisters' petition to remove Balthus's canvas reads) seems to aim at an organization of the art exhibition within the logic of a "safe space." If the images confront us with feelings we can't bear and will make us explode in insult or triggered injury, we need to be protected from them. But who issues the safety certificate? Clearly the relations between art and the masses, the way they were established since the nineteenth century, are in flux again today. An old question vehemently returns—is art for the many or the few?

The dissolving of art into the circulation of images in the world ushers a confusion between literality and a figurative, metaphoric language. But the form of the painting is its content. Art is insinuated with totalitarian requirements that it does not and should not possess. To argue against the subjunctive, to replace the figurative with the literal, means disguising a power struggle in a dispute that is neither ethical nor aesthetic, only political.

3 *Un quadro con un Amore ridente in atto di dispregiare il mondo* (a painting of a laughing Amor, full of scorn for the world) was found in the painting's caption in Vincenzo Giustiniani's inventory.

4 Some of the standard trophies representing the seven liberal arts of proper intellectual learning. Since medieval times, these were comprised of the three arts of the trivium: grammar, logic, and rhetoric; and the four arts of the quadrivium: geometry, arithmetic, astronomy, and music.

Susanna and the Elders (1647) by Rembrandt van Rijn

A young woman is about to step into the water. She directs her worried gaze at us while her naked body leans forward. Her fair skin glows in a ray of light, illuminating the right side of *Susanna and the Elders* by Rembrandt van Rijn, an oil on panel painting. She has just doffed her opulent gown in warm reds, placed behind her with a pair of crimson slippers. The warmth of the ankles that have just left them is almost palpable. She is about to bathe, and her right foot, stable and fleshy, is already in the clear water. Her gaze makes us her witness as an elegantly dressed older man grabs the fabric barely cloaking her unguarded back with one hand; the other supports his wrinkled face. Another elder painted in less detail accompanies him; his bearded face is lit in a sealed expression as both sneak on a stony staircase behind their jolted, defenseless prey.

Conspiracy and libel lie at the core of the story told in the Book of Daniel of the virtuous young wife of a wealthy Babylonian Jew. Threatened with blackmail by two distinguished judges were she not to sleep with them, Susanna put her trust in God and refused their proposition. They defamed her, claiming she was meeting a lover at the bath. She was to be put to death for promiscuity when the young Daniel saved her.

The story was popular in a seventeenth-century Amsterdam that saw, as a result of Calvinist iconoclasm, the banishment of most art from churches, including religious-themed paintings. Such Biblical scenes were now painted to be shown in the domestic, secular sphere, where they were tolerated and in fact flourished. *Susanna* is imbued with a peculiar tension between spiritual passion and quotidian life that many of Rembrandt's paintings, and others of the Dutch Golden Age, share as a result of this disposition.[1] Nowhere in the biblical plot is there mention of bathing or physical assault, but like other biblical or mythological narrations with female protagonists, the theme had served as a qualified smokescreen for showing the (erotic) nude endorsed by virtue in art since the sixteenth century.

Prosperity presented a moral ambiguity that plagued the culture of the Netherlands, whose economy had emerged to dominate the world by the mid-seventeenth century. The country became a global empire. Its wealth and conspicuous consumption—of Ming porcelain, Lyon silk, Brazilian emeralds, Oriental spices, and other wordly treasures—merged with the restraints of Calvinist inhibition and shame.[2] In fewer than one hundred years, the tiny nation with a population of less than two million had overcome a flood that almost drowned the low landscape, as well as an eighty-year war against Spain. It was with the consciousness of a chosen people whose residues are still evident today. How to be strong, yet pure? How to be rich, yet humble?

Rembrandt was forty-one years old when the painting was completed in 1647, twelve years after his first sketches of the motif around 1635. The painting process seems to have been laborious and accompanied by a dynamic exchange of ideas within the studio. Numerous drawings and sketches and an earlier painting hanging in Berlin testify to a continuous, exceptionally long preoccupation with the subject. In *Susanna Harassed by the Elders* (after 1636, attributed to his workshop) the naked back of Susanna, this time crouching and with unkempt hair, is so fair and bright it neutralizes her dark surroundings like a light source; an earlier *Susanna* (1636, now in Mauritshuis in The Hague) features a delicately cropped version of the scene as it appears in Berlin, with the nude woman isolated and facing the artist and viewer; the older men, well disguised and hardly recognizable, hide in the bushes.

But what was his true subject? As an artist and a workshop director, Rembrandt kept returning to the moment of undressing, of a woman preparing to bathe. The later *Bathsheba* (1654, now in the Louvre

1 Such dispositions between sanctuaries and domestic interiors or landscapes may have later informed northern European modern art, particularly that of Vincent van Gogh, Piet Mondrian, Wassily Kandinsky, or Kasimir Malevich.
2 See Simon Schama, *The Embarrassment of Riches. An Interpretation of Dutch Culture in the Golden Age* (New York, 1987).

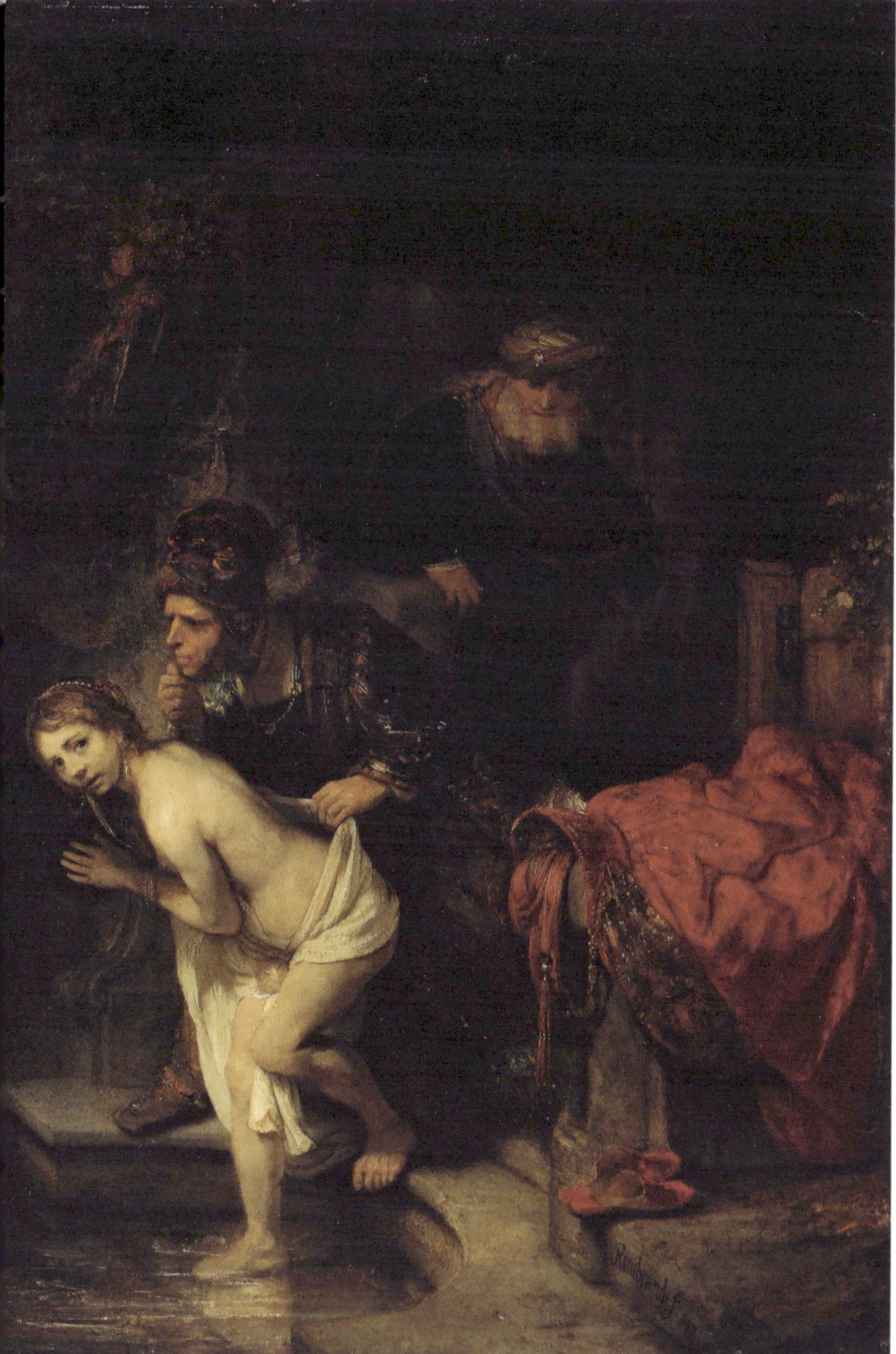

Museum in Paris) and *A Woman Bathing in a Stream* (also 1654, now in the National Gallery in London) can be added to this accumulating, quite specific attempt. Different from depictions of bathing women as scopophilic imagery, Rembrandt seems more invested in capturing this instant of a woman's exposing her nakedness, acknowledging the power relations in which the artist is also an observer interrupting a private moment. It is a moment in which shame, awareness, and temptation dissolve into each other.[3] It is not a mere objectification of the woman by the Elders, the painter, and consequently the viewer; Rembrandt rather depicts a moment of interruption of a private circuit; a disruption of the woman's presence to herself. The moment also exposes a disintegration; her split from herself is a fundamental one.[4] Pieter Lastman's *Susanna and the Elders*'s influence on Rembrandt's composition is evident; both paintings hang at the Gemäldegalerie today. But while Lastman's *Susanna* (1614) seems like a theatrical, high-resolution choreography within a naturalistic garden in which gazes seem aimed at nothing or nobody, Rembrandt's fills its viewer with paralyzing terror. Shame and pity intertwine in viewing Susanna's hopeless situation, trapped in a virile ambush as a tangible human presence made of paint.

The look in Susanna's eyes may reveal a sense of intimacy between model and artist. It was most probably Hendrickje Stoffels modeling for Rembrandt as Susanna in his studio, assuming his late wife Saskia's role. Often using the women who were most important in his personal life as models, Rembrandt was introducing interiority and privacy into a public space: the studio and the canvas. He was already a widower for six years by the time the painting was completed, following what in all accounts seemed to be not only a socially advantageous marriage but a loving relationship with Saskia. She had died when their only surviving son, Titus, was a baby. Twenty years the artist's junior, Stoffels would soon become his mistress and later give birth to their daughter Cornelia, named after Rembrandt's mother.

3 "Shame is the most isolating of feelings but also the most primitive of social responses ... simultaneously the discovery of the isolation of the individual, his presence to himself, but also to others." Stanley Cavell, *Must We Mean What We Say?* (Chicago, 1976), p. 286.
4 Joan Copjec, "The Object-Gaze: Shame, Hejab, Cinema," in *Filozofski vestnik* (Vol. XXVII, 2006).

The two openly lived together, but he never married her for the sake of his late wife's inheritance. Stoffels would be candidly featured in several of Rembrandt's later most distinctive depictions of women, specifically *Bathsheba* (1654). This possibly caused the Amsterdam Church Council to summon her the same year to answer a charge of "living in whoredom" with Rembrandt.

It is thus easy to imagine her identification with the harassed and exposed woman informing Susanna's enduring expression in the painting. Stoffels was repeatedly hounded by Amsterdam church and courts, but remained by Rembrandt's side until her death seven years before his, caring for him when his popularity among clients and dealers waned and he, bankrupted yet not unaware of his supremacy as a painter, became her and his son's "employee" before the law. This kind of depiction of women evoked critical outrage even in Rembrandt's lifetime. Why would he deliberately choose to represent vulgar peasant women instead of a Greek Venus? Andries Pels, a Dutch poet, wrote in 1681, "Pendulous breasts, distorted hands, even the marks of the corset laces over the belly, or the garter about the leg: all had to be shown if Nature was to have her due. He wouldn't listen to rules or reasons of moderation in showing parts of the body."[5] Rembrandt's "notions of the delicate forms of women would have frightened an Arctic bear," the British author Benjamin Robert Haydon wrote in the *Encyclopaedia Britannica* in 1838. Undoubtedly it is always a particular woman modeling for the artist in his studio. Rembrandt introduced to painting a female nude that is neither an ideal monument nor a source of voyeuristic pleasure, but rather incarnated through uncompromising naturalism that spares us no detail. His nudes are nevertheless affectionate and desiring, a contradictory condition ungraspable to several writers even today, even when defending Rembrandt's portrayal of women. To this day, the very inclination of art-historical writers (for example Kenneth Clark, and later, Simon Schama) seems too infected with bias.[6]

Yet being the ultimate allegory, the female nude had been an infinitely fecund formative principle to masculine Western art in

5 Simon Schama, "Rembrandt and Women," *Bulletin of the American Academy of Arts and Sciences*, (Vol. 38, No. 7, April 1985), pp. 21–47.

modern times, serving both the artist's desire and his reflection on the conventions of painting. Corpulent and sublime, ideal and obscene, the female nude, from Rembrandt to Marcel Duchamp, is always also painting itself. As long as the history of Western art was dictated by men, the female nude also always served as a projection screen; a manifold allegorical body of painting.

On the canvas surface, the painted light dims as it moves away from the picture's highlight, Susanna. The rest of the painting, considered to be one of Rembrandt's masterpieces within the relatively rich collection at the Gemäldegalerie, is slightly smeared—a brown-green, grossly incomplete palace architecture and vegetation surrounding the garden pond. Although the painting, as it was acquired in 1883 by the Gemäldegalerie in Berlin, was praised by the art historian and critic Adolf Rosenberg as "much spared from any damage or an unknown intervening hand," something feels strange about it. The thick impasto is present and tactile; the organization of light seems at first typical: Rembrandt applied chiaroscuro to provide emphasis in a picture. He "lit" to create a dramatic effect not necessarily according to a proper physical representation until gradually, in later paintings, light and shadow released themselves from the picture and served the ends of painting itself. But the gross details here, the overwhelmingly murky two-thirds of the ground surface surrounding the three figures, lend the impression that the painting was dipped in a green sauce.

The painting's awkwardness was ratified and expounded with a sensational discovery in 2015 by the Gemäldegalerie's team, when Katja Kleinert, Curator for Dutch and Flemish Art of the 17th Century, and conservator Claudia Laurenze-Landsberg turned Rosenberg's enthusiastic 1883 assessment upside down. The painting was probably sold the year it was completed. In the eighteenth century it then found its way to the collection of Sir Joshua Reynolds (1723–92). The ambitious painter and founding president of the Royal Academy

6 Attack and defense alike had blinded them from recognizing what Gustave Courbet would show some 200 years after Rembrandt, depicting what no modern (Western) painter has before him as a revealing of an origin of everything, of truth of painting itself.

purchased the painting through his friend, the author and conservative politician Edmund Burke.

When looking at Richard Earlom's 1769 mezzotint print of *Susanna*, which was made just as the painting arrived in Reynolds's collection and now also hangs in Berlin, we now can confirm that Reynolds restored, intervened, and in fact completely erased and extensively altered most of Rembrandt's original painting. X-ray and pigment analysis followed the comparison with the copy and resulted in this rather shocking revelation: apparently, Reynolds, who possessed an impressive art collection comprising works by masters of Roman, Florentine, Bolognese, Venetian, French, Flemish, and Dutch schools (including twenty-seven Rembrandts, and several works each by Bellini, Titian, Velázquez, and Rubens) adjusted, and in fact altered, many of them.

In the case of *Susanna*, as the team in the Gemäldegalerie supported by the Reynolds Research Project in the United Kingdom found out, Reynolds was extremely assertive in his modifications. "It is very rare to see a picture of any great painter that has not been defaced and mended by picture-cleaners and been reduced by that means to half its value," he said,[7] criticizing contemporary interventions and clarifying his focus on value improvement and enhancement. Few areas on the canvas remain untouched by the curious, experimental master. His passion for improving the painting and making it more Rembrandt-like resulted in a darker, browner color palette in a much coarser and less detailed background. Entire parts of the garden were eliminated and replaced with new details. Two escaping figures of Susanna's maids painted by Rembrandt were completely concealed within the smudged ground. Stereoscope recordings show that Reynolds covered delicate brushstroke details by Rembrandt in the garden and clothing. Perhaps he wanted to update the relations between background and figures, clarifying the focus on the painting's story or content through the three subjects in the front. Most profound is Reynolds's transformation of the face of the bearded elder at the back bedrock staircase. According to Earlom's copy,

7 David Bomford, "Picture Cleaning: Positivism and Metaphysics," in *The Conservation of Easel Paintings*, eds. Joyce Hill Stoner and Rebecca Rushfield (Oxford and New York, 2012), p. 485.

Rembrandt's elder possessed a repellent, leering expression with an open mouth and bared teeth. Reynolds soothed the expression, closing the man's mouth and granting him a smug grin.

Luckily, Reynolds left the figure of Susanna almost untouched. Maybe he was satisfied with Rembrandt's take. We can imagine she looks at us very much like she would have 300 years ago, but not so the rest of the painting. Reynolds's reworking, almost inconceivable today, may have been an exceptional case of diligence.[8] But it also speaks to a shift in the location of the origin of the artwork's authority. Reynolds's overidentification is with the *painting* (i.e. the artwork), treating it as a paintable surface, rather than with the *painter* (i.e. the artist). It seems to be prompted by the idea that *art* is bigger than its executors or authors. And that he, Reynolds, should liberate the painting from the limitation of a singular artist, in this case Rembrandt (or his workshop) for the sake of good art. Good art as such, as he understands it, is the source of authority calling him to act.

Since the painting's transition from the private collection of the painter (who sought to establish a British Renaissance on his own in eighteenth-century London) to the royal, later national museum collection in nineteenth-century Berlin, the coordinates determining the artwork's value have changed. The current scientific autopsy of the artwork documenting its plot and evaluating its provenance seeks to detect and authenticate its creator. The encyclopedic container that is the museum tries not only to attribute *Susanna* to Rembrandt, but also to restore the artwork an aura whose locus has been shifted.

Ironically, the painting that evolves around conspiracy and slander like the Biblical story that is its subject, has been violated itself. Not only has the woman's body, as it is to itself and its un-seenness,

8 The recent multimillion-euro public restoration process of Rembrandt's *The Night Watch* (1642), performed live and streamed online from the Rijksmuseum in Amsterdam as of July 2019, showcases the evolution of art spectatorship and the emphasis on originality in the artwork since Reynolds's time in the eighteenth century. The painting that was commissioned by the leader of Amsterdam's civic guard, marking the height of Rembrandt's career (at a time in which his personal life was probably falling to pieces) was cut on all sides in 1715 in order to fit through two doors on the second floor of the Nieuwe Stadhuis. Today, as research collides with tourism and entertainment, the artwork is reestablished as something at once spectacular and sacred.

been intruded upon, but also the artist's original intentions. Susanna's physical exposure points to the cover-up that is the painting. The more we look at it, the less we know what we are seeing.

Joseph Accused by Potiphar's Wife (1655) by Rembrandt van Rijn

Darkness envelops the protagonists of the medium-format painting by Rembrandt van Rijn titled *Joseph Accused by Potiphar's Wife*. Our eyes are drawn to Potiphar's wife, sitting on the corner of a bed, her fleshy décolletage exposed. Tactile layers of light-hued paint illuminate the figure. One of her hands touches her breast, which is partly covered by an opulent reddish robe. Her other hand is pulled toward the viewer, outside the canvas, in a forceful gesture that is inviting, persuasive, and threatening. She seems to be intimating a story, performing seduction. To her left is Potiphar, wearing a decorated Oriental turban. To her right, across the bed, we see Joseph's bowing figure; the palm of his hand, which seems unfinished, is held toward the couple as if to say, "No!"

A Calvinist reader of the Bible, Rembrandt chose seldom-depicted biblical scenes as a framework for several pictures. Such is the case with the story of Joseph and Potiphar's wife. It was a less popular topos than *Susanna and the Elders* (1647), another of the Gemäldegalerie's sixteen paintings by Rembrandt. The biblical story tells us of a wealthy man's wife, Potiphar, who tries to entice Joseph, the handsome Hebrew servant, sold off by his envious brothers and who has brought blessings to Potiphar's house. As she tries to force him to lie in her bed, grasping for his clothing, he manages to escape, leaving his gown in her hands. This in return serves as her fabricated evidence for the sexual act. When Potiphar returns, she shows him Joseph's gown and accuses Joseph of raping her. Joseph is then jailed, an initially unfortunate situation that will eventually advance him to the Pharaoh's court.

Both the aforementioned Susanna and Potiphar's wife embody acts of undressing and covering. The biblical story of Susanna was often used in painting as an opportunity to depict a female nude. In all

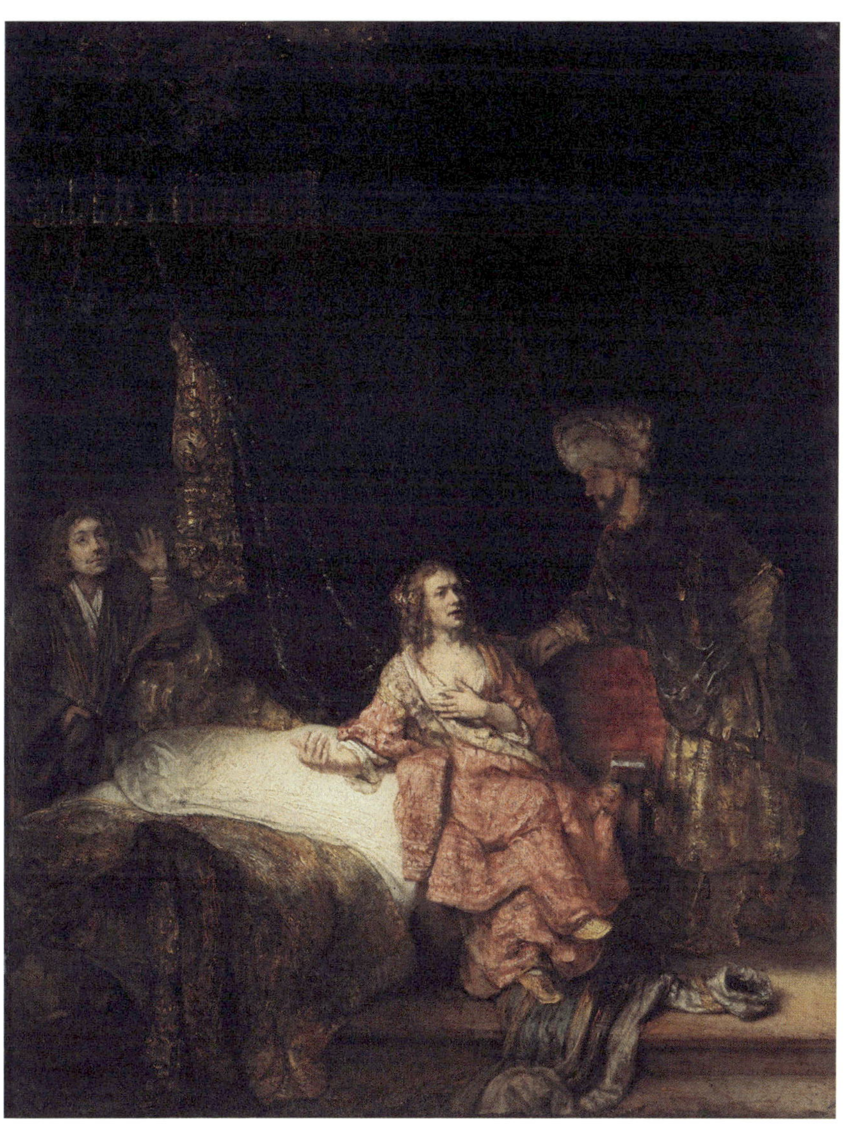

his variations of the scene, Rembrandt chose to turn the viewer's gaze to witness the embarrassment that comes with disrobing while being watched. Yet while Susanna is caught naked, her body inclined in shame, Potiphar's wife strips the young man who rejects her. The story unfolds an exceptional inversion or role reversal, making the man the victim, a position usually reserved for women. Moreover, it ascribes attributes of femininity to Joseph's figure, and masculine features to Potiphar's wife. While he is described as beautiful and beloved ("and Joseph was of beautiful form, and fair to look upon"), [1] she is demanding and ready to strike. He guards his innocence and refrains from surrender. She is the powerful wife of the house's master; he is a slave. She is established and indigenous; he is young and foreign. He is punished, although he is innocent.

Several contemporaneous depictions of this biblical attempted rape involve swift movements, contact between the man and the woman, and nudity. Such is the case in both of Guido Reni's paintings on the subject (from 1626 and 1630), in which the two figures touch each other. Jacopo Tintoretto (1555) has Potiphar's wife lying completely naked, entangled in an acrobatic gesture to pull on the gown. Even Rembrandt's earlier drawing of the scene shows a physical struggle between the dressed young man and the large woman lying in her canopied bed, her spread legs uncompromisingly expose her lower belly and groin. In the painting *Joseph Accused by Potiphar's Wife*, though, the composition is altogether static and seems to feature merely one protagonist: Potiphar's wife. Instead of undressing Joseph, she steps on his torn gown.

Three superimposed upside-down triangles dominate Rembrandt's composition and allude almost too bluntly to feminine sexuality—are they inverted to evoke the female sex, which more closely approximates the shape of a "V" than the Greek letter Delta? The first, formed by Potiphar's wife's neckline and garment, indicates her sex; the second is formed by the sheets in a similar white hue; its apex is in the painting's middle foreground. The third comprises the illuminated faces of Joseph and the accusing woman. Its vertex appears at another point of light on the folds of her garment, as it were, between her knees.

1 Genesis 39:6.

Triangles recur in Renaissance compositions, indicating spatial depth. Whereas Rembrandt's paintings (and Baroque artworks in general; their contribution to rendering a new mode of representation starting with Caravaggio) are much more concerned with a dramatic peak—initially the last ray of light, ideally falling on Christ's head—and are structured through diagonals. The "V" shapes here therefore seem odd or atypical. It is almost as though their apexes attempt to pin down the essence of female sexuality and we, the viewers, are implicated in perceiving the scene through three superimposed evocations of it. There also seems to be a contrivance at work imposing a distortion, just like any accusation does, affecting whom we choose to believe: the accused or the accuser. The painting's spatial organization and its illuminated indicators evoke the possibility that this distorted and restricted prism of perception could also be that to which the male protagonists have equally succumbed.

Yet the core of this painting lies neither in the wife, in her textiles, corpulence, and intentional expression, nor in the slightly obscured companions. The peak of this painting's drama is rather Potiphar's bed, covered with white sheets, a scene of a crime that did not take place, a radiant, shimmering paint stain that is almost abstract in nature. Like in *Susanna and the Elders*, the picture narrates a conspiracy, a libel, a lie about an act of carnal nature. In both paintings, the subject around which the picture revolves takes the shape of a void. Both women seem to touch their own skin; Potiphar's wife does so with theatricality and an expression of hurt pride.

But her touching goes beyond hypocritical virtue. It seems to be closing a circuit, as though the painting were touching itself. Half-bare, half-dressed, what she unveils, what she is in fact the revelation of, is both secret and lie—the act of concealment that is painting itself. What we see is the appearance of a concealing that inseparably belongs to both the feminine and visible realms. Her intrigue is painting's own conspiracy. The classic Greek tale of the contest between painters Zeuxis and Parrhasius tells us of two strategies of painterly deception: Zeuxis paints grapes that attract birds, but Parrhasius wins by painting a veil on the wall so lifelike that Zeuxis asks him what lies behind it. While animals are fooled by the appearance of reality, humans are deceived by the veil, which not only imitates reality, but also obscures it. The gaze is enticed to look for what is behind the veil. The human way of deception is lure and temptation.[2]

Perhaps this has to do with the fact that nudes are not a major component of Rembrandt's oeuvre, compared to artists such as Titian or Peter Paul Rubens. Rembrandt's paintings are laden with draperies, textiles, veils, robes, clothing, and covers that enfold, surround, or wrap his protagonists in thick, abundant, tactile layers of fabric and paint that obscure the naked body. They keep these men's and women's bodies a precarious, ephemeral creation that is never completely stable or static, like a curtain that is fleetingly raised, only to drop back down. Unmistakably incorporated into the canvas upon which they are painted, the figures and objects inhabiting Rembrandt's paintings are protected from optical description, whose violence Rembrandt emphasizes in *The Anatomy Lesson of Dr. Nicolaes Tulp* (1632), by showing us the scientific dissection as a sacrifice of the body in favor of the corpse. He is perhaps already aware of it being the consequence of the Cartesian slicing of being into a body and a soul, separated.

Much more than the work of hard-edged lines and rigid contours, Rembrandt shaped his forms with light, color, and thick layers of paint. Abandoning classicist purity and avoiding the aid of symbolism, he conjures up the inner life of surfaces, including human bodies and faces. His charged brushstrokes turn the painting against the picture. In a radical move, he transfers painting's gravity from its pictorial content to the painting's surface itself. He opens a possibility for the medium to become not pictorial. This is why almost any modern painter (J.M.W. Turner, Eugene Delacroix, and Vincent van Gogh, but also Chaim Soutine, Frank Auerbach, maybe even Francis Bacon) "took himself for Rembrandt," as Pablo Picasso famously proclaimed to his lover Françoise Gilot. This was the beginning, or at least *one* beginning, of modern painting eventually getting rid of the object completely and moving into its nonobjective and antipictorial fulfilment.

A dark density on the canvas in *Joseph Accused by Potiphar's Wife* swallows the bed's canopy and about two-thirds of the painting's surface, which is sporadically punctured by glittering marks of golden

2 "A triumph of the gaze over the eye." See Jacques Lacan, *The Four Fundamental Concepts of Psycho-Analysis* (London, 1979), pp. 103, 112; see also Mladen Dolar, *A Voice and Nothing More* (Cambridge, MA and London, 2006).

garments and metallic ornaments. These are painted in thick self-manifested brushstrokes. Within this dark space, pigments were identified as Prussian Blue, the first modern synthetic pigment. This colorfast, economical color would become a practical, popular replacement for the elaborate and expensive blue pigments painters had used until then, like the ultramarine made of the precious stone lapis lazuli. However, Prussian Blue was synthesized in Berlin for the first time about fifty years after this painting was signed, and thirty-seven years after Rembrandt's death.

Forensic research of the painting carried out until today testifies to an extensive and rough restoration that the painting must have undergone in the eighteen-thirties. The Berlin team has not yet issued a final verdict. Furthermore, plenty of details attest to multiple instances of overpainting and retouching. The figures of Potiphar and Joseph seem divergent for Rembrandt; perhaps we are dealing with a painting executed by Rembrandt's workshop. Indeed, they seem to be influenced by miniatures from the Indian-Mughal Empire, which Rembrandt may have seen and by which he perhaps sought to convey "Oriental" attributes. Was Rembrandt also aware of the Oriental transfiguration in this story? While Potiphar's wife bears no name in the Hebrew Bible, she later appears in the Quran, and thereafter in Persian and Indian traditions, as Zulaikha. Her desire for Joseph/Yusuf is depicted in these traditions as a passion for beauty rather than the Protestant highlighting of slander, female sexuality's evil, and abstinence.

This painting's captivation is thus made even more complicated. How much of what we see is influenced by what we project upon it? The attributions of Rembrandt's works have been questioned many times since the early twentieth century. From an estimated 1,000 paintings, research has so far managed to assign other authorship, mostly to students and his workshop, to more than half of them. Paradoxically, Rembrandt has left us forever puzzled, unable to distinguish between his individual genius and the effects of individuality, which he perfected and bequeathed to his students and apprentices during his long and prolific undertaking.

Through a Glass Wall

Woman with a Pearl Necklace (1663–65) by Jan Vermeer

About to end her morning toilette, the woman who raises her arms to don a necklace in Jan Vermeer's *Woman with a Pearl Necklace* fills the right side of the rather small canvas. Immobile, she gleams as though the entirety of her being—red ribbon, pearl earrings, fair skin—depends on the light entering from the window. Trimmed with ermine, her yellow robe echoes the color of the curtain, rolled to the side of the window; an aperture to the light. It coats her, as does the lucent, almost breathing wall that the picture's main plane and absorbs our gaze.

As much as her facing the light is charged with a sense of holiness; as much as her cleansing tools may serve an allegory for the purification of the soul, they are ultimately profane. She could be an earthly transfiguration of a Venus being born (the pearls would speak for that); or a Bathsheba at her bath preparing herself for the king. On the wooden table, underneath the mirror, a silver basin shimmers like the pearls in her necklace. Across the way, an empty leather chair's metal pins, facing us diagonally, glint as though they, too, were delicate gemstones. A small powder brush—we can almost count its bristles—is laid close to a flat rectangular comb, so casually real that one almost wants to pick it up. The mundane and the sacred are the ends that hold Vermeer's painting: his is an ascetic theology of the quotidian.

Two paintings by Vermeer hang in Berlin amid other seventeenth-century Dutch Masters works. The artist belonged to the third generation of this Golden Age; his themes were almost always within one of its great conventions: pictures of everyday life and ordinary people. But against the picturesque, fluent, free, and descriptive qualities of what was later dubbed Genre Painting, Vermeer's approach stands

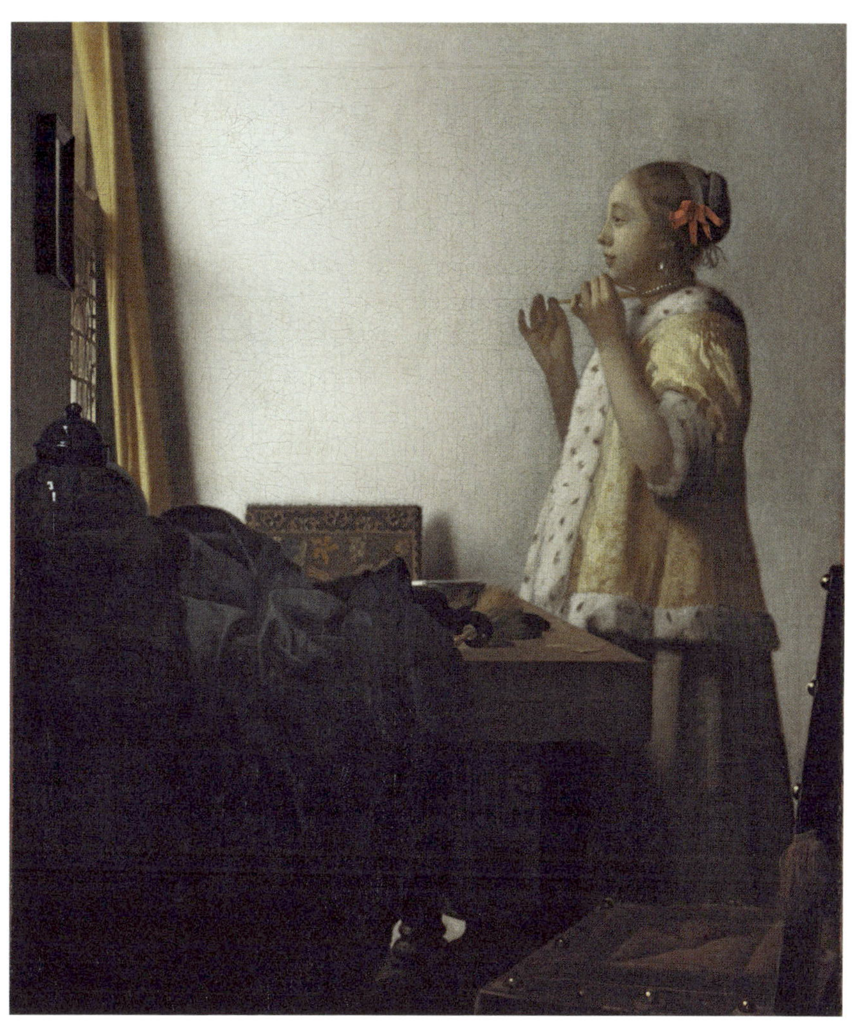

out as an empirical study that aspires to be methodically objective. The two paintings display, in a way, a summarized evolution in the middle of the artist's path to refinement.

In the earlier *The Wine Glass* (1658–60), a man and a woman appear at an inn's table set with delicate abundances. A checkered tile floor, an Oriental carpet on the table, and a chair furnish the painting in the pervasive geometry of three-dimensional perspective. In contrast to the almost tactile emptiness that fills *Woman with a Pearl Necklace*, with the wall claiming almost two-thirds of the canvas, the room in *The Wine Glass* is decorated with a landscape painting and a colored stained-glass window that, with the carpet on the table, offer a pattern within a pattern, a picture within a picture. Yet the human activity looks mummified and frozen. The man and woman seem part of a still life; the painting's tapestry.

In Vermeer, this inhibition and restraint from getting closer, from describing life, finds a form in the *Necklace* and subsequent works, according to Lawrence Gowing's remarkable study of the artist.[1] It is a certain split of the artist's protocoling gaze that always activates detachment and love at the same time. Vermeer painted several other "pearl pictures" around the time of the *Necklace*. Their compositions surround a woman unguarded, held still while captivated in a minute activity and illuminated by daylight poured into the space like an ethereal cloud. In the *Necklace*, against this feminine verticality rooted in the floor, the darker, lower part of the painting has a sharp horizontal corner of a table and an empty chair that serve as a barrier separating us (and the painter) from what we see. This recurs in Vermeer's oeuvre: chairs, curtains, tables, and finally the artist himself with his back to us in *The Art of Painting* (1666–68) stand in the foreground to hold us at a distance from what we perceive, and what we, and he, perhaps desire, but remains beyond contact.

It is easy to imagine how the founders of the collection inhabiting the Gemäldegalerie today—involving their personal preferences with the national pedagogic mission to create a significant scholarly collection for Prussia to succeed the royal collections of Frederick William of Brandenburg and Frederick the Great (as any establish-

1 Lawrence Gowing, *Vermeer* (London, 1997 [1952]).

ment of a collection shows)—much favored Rembrandt over Vermeer. They didn't care much about acquiring the rare works of the other Dutch master, which were then perhaps still available. Vermeer's limited oeuvre comprises about thirty-six paintings—a number that is hardly half of Rembrandt's self-portraits.

Vermeer, a shortened form of Van der Meer (from the sea), was the name the artist inherited from his hardworking father, a silk weaver, art dealer, and innkeeper who probably invented his last name. And although much about the painter's life could have been known all along, he was designated by his rediscoverers toward the end of the nineteenth century to be born from the sea as a modern artist—son of wind and water, in correlation to his surname. Vermeer was described as the "Sphinx of Delft" by the French art critic Théophile Thoré, who referred to the lack of written history of the artist, and the enigmatic quality of his work. In 1866 under the pseudonym Wilhelm Bürger, Thoré claimed to have rescued the painter from obscurity. In his other role as an exhibition maker and collector, Thoré-Bürger owned several Vermeers, among them *Woman with a Pearl Necklace*, for about eight years.

Vermeer was born in Delft as Jan Vermeer and changed his first name to Johannes when he, age twenty-one, married Catherine Bolnes, a Catholic from Gouda with a mother of means. The couple joined the small Catholic minority amidst the Calvinist-Protestant city, where Vermeer remained until his death in 1675 at age forty-three. His early artistic training remains a mystery. He must have had access to some of the leading artists in Delft through his father's network. He also dealt in art, following his father's trade. Yet nowhere in Vermeer's paintings can we figure out what kind of man he was.[2]

It was precisely Vermeer's oblivion, which Thoré-Bürger claimed to undo, that became proof of the artist's modernity. "We go to him," Gustave Vanzype wrote in a 1908 monograph, "because a sort of mysterious prescience made him see as we see, made him discern, divine, and anticipate a sensibility that would not develop until two centuries

2 Speculations have often arisen on the artist's connection to Rene Descartes's turn inward and the institution of the subject, and even a correlation to Baruch Spinoza's immanency of world and God. Both thinkers were close to him geographically and historically.

after him."[3] The monograph was also owned by Marcel Proust, who famously sent his art-critic protagonist Bergotte in *In Search of Lost Time* (1913–22) to collapse and die, comprehending the failure of his own work, facing *The View of Delft* (1660–61) in Paris as an ultimate act of beholding an artwork. Looking for a little yellow piece of wall (*petit pan*) he had previously overlooked in the painting and that he'd learned of from another writer, Bergotte (Proust) summarizes Vermeer's endeavor: the yellow piece of wall was everything and nothing, an absolute mundane detail that is fundamentally prinicipal.[4]

Perhaps what Vanzype, Proust, and Thoré-Bürger responded to and understood as modern was a gaze recovered from Vermeer's paintings; one that was engaged in a movement outward and inward at the same time. He seems to not know or care what he is painting, as though the conceptual world of what a thing is—a finger, a nose, a table—is converted to a depiction committed merely to the light that falls upon it. Vermeer's optical detachment is idiosyncratic but completely impersonal and predates retinal Impressionism. His aloof gaze, recording things as they appear before our eyes to the point of their obscurity and certainly seen as eccentric in his time, anticipates photography.

Upon his visit to Holland in 1874, Henry James noted in his journal the confusion between the reality he saw and its image in Dutch paintings: "… when you are looking at the copies, you seem to be looking at the originals. Is it a canal-side in Haarlem, or is it a Van der Heyden? … The maid-servants in the streets seem to have stepped out of the frame of a Gerard Dow, and appear equally adapted for stepping back again."[5] Johann Wolfgang von Goethe too, describes in his autobiography how, after wandering out of the Dresden Gemäldegalerie into the shoemaker's workshop where he was living, the paintings he had

3 See Joseph Leo Koerner, "First Among Equals," *The New York Review of Books* (February 2019).
4 Proust was obsessed with Vermeer ever since he saw *The View of Delft* in The Hague, "the most beautiful painting in the world," and intended to write his own study of the painter. See Lea Dovev, *Six Modes of Painting-Music* (Jerusalem, 2003) pp. 194–230.
5 Henry James, *Transatlantic Sketches* (Boston, 1875), p. 382.

seen reverberated; he could hardly believe his eyes at the perfection of a painting by Ostade.[6]

Within the style defined as naturalistic, one can find contradicting drives—to describe, to map, to imitate and reflect like a mirror, and to deceive (trompe l'oeil, for example). Svetlana Alpers defines northern descriptive art as one in which the world precedes the artist. Conversely, in the southern (Italian) storytelling art, the sovereign artist precedes the world and constitutes it according to his point of view.[7] Vermeer undoubtedly belongs to his time and place and many records attest to his influence by fellow contemporary artists, but his take on description is a reflective one that attains the limits of giving an account, of showing what there is, if we follow Alpers's division.

We can see why the question pointed out in James's report from Holland, or Goethe's confusion between image and life—namely, where is the art?—is probably the wrong one to be asked with Vermeer. Articulating their puzzling over the descriptive character of seventeenth-century Dutch painting precedes questions regarding technological images today. If images are situated on the threshold of the physical world and our perception of it, what kind of art is it? Vermeer's art is modern by means of a glass wall he sets that separates us from what we observe (or, emphasizes this separation and thus allows an intimacy with it). His is a gaze that behaves like both a machine and a god. It renders the question obsolete whether the painter, who was surrounded by lenses and fascinated with optical devices, was in fact using a camera obscura for his paintings.[8] What interested him in the optical device was the approach it mandates.

The woman in the painting holds the two ribbons of her pearl necklace apart just before closing it, the opening of the hands lets the light in, as if she were made to show how it falls on things. For

6 See Johann Wolfgang von Goethe, *Truth and Poetry: From My Life*, ed. Parke Godwin (New York, 1846 [1811–13]).
7 See Svetlana Alpers, *The Art of Describing: Dutch Art in the Seventeenth Century* (Chicago, 1983). Or, in Ernst Gombrich's words, "the Northeners have their brains in their hands while Italians have them in their heads." *Norm and Form* (London, 1966), p.115.
8 His contemporary in Delft and later executor of will, and possibly the model for *The Astronomer* and *The Geographer* (*Der Astronom*, 1668, in the Louvre, and *Der Geograph*, 1668–1669, in the Städel Museum) was Anthony van Leeuwenhoek, a Dutch pioneer of optic studies.

his slightly older wife, Vermeer relinquished his family religion. The couple probably moved in with Cathcrine's dominant, wealthy mother in Delft.[9] This house, where he would paint all of his known paintings, was likely inhabited mostly by females (besides his wife and her mother, there were eleven children, among them seven girls). Surrounded thus by a household of women, the world he repeatedly depicted in his paintings—closed, untroubled and yet other, incomprehensible, and even sublime—aligned completely with the feminine.

The window and mirror the woman faces offer her the two possibilities of painting: a mirroring reflection or a window to look through. Our gaze at the wall intersects with her gaze observing herself. Both lead to a perspectival void.

9 Maria Thins welcomed Vermeer into her family despite his less prominent social background. She must have considered this approval seriously, since her own marriage was abusive and violent.

Prince Heinrich Lubomirski as the Genius of Fame (1787–88) by Élisabeth Vigée-Lebrun

A painting, beaming with warm colors, was recently pulled out of storage to hang in a temporary exhibition between works by Peter Paul Rubens, Jean-Antoine Watteau, and Joshua Reynolds. It shows a winged boy kneeling in a pose that recalls a classic crouching Venus-Aphrodite. In his hand he holds a myrtle wreath, a symbol of innocence, love, and glory. A red stole falls elegantly on soft, fleshy legs, hardly concealing the naked androgynous body. The childish face is turned to his side, passing over the viewer, staring into the space with self-absorption. Two feathery wings grow from the boy's back. The wooden surface grants the oil painting's hues a certain brightness and gloss, making the boy's skin radiant; red lips echoing the velvety scarlet cloth.

Painted in the summer of 1789 by Élisabeth Vigée-Lebrun in Paris, the child model, Prince Henryk Lubomirski, was part of the entourage to a princess escaping Poland in revolutionary times. The heirless princess abducted the handsome child, a distant relative of hers, at a young age and raised him as her son. A detail in the plain gray-blue studio background disrupts the painting's harmony: a quiver with arrows at the boy's feet that may hint at the events already starting to take shape that summer that would eventually escalate to revolution, forcing the resourceful and sober painter to leave her homeland with her daughter and extend her exceptional career abroad for twelve years, because of her association with French queen Marie Antoinette.

Vigée-Lebrun traveled to Italy, where in 1790 she was elected to membership in the Accademia di San Luca in Rome. She worked in Florence, Naples, Vienna, Saint Petersburg, and Berlin before returning to France, taking sittings from members of the royal families

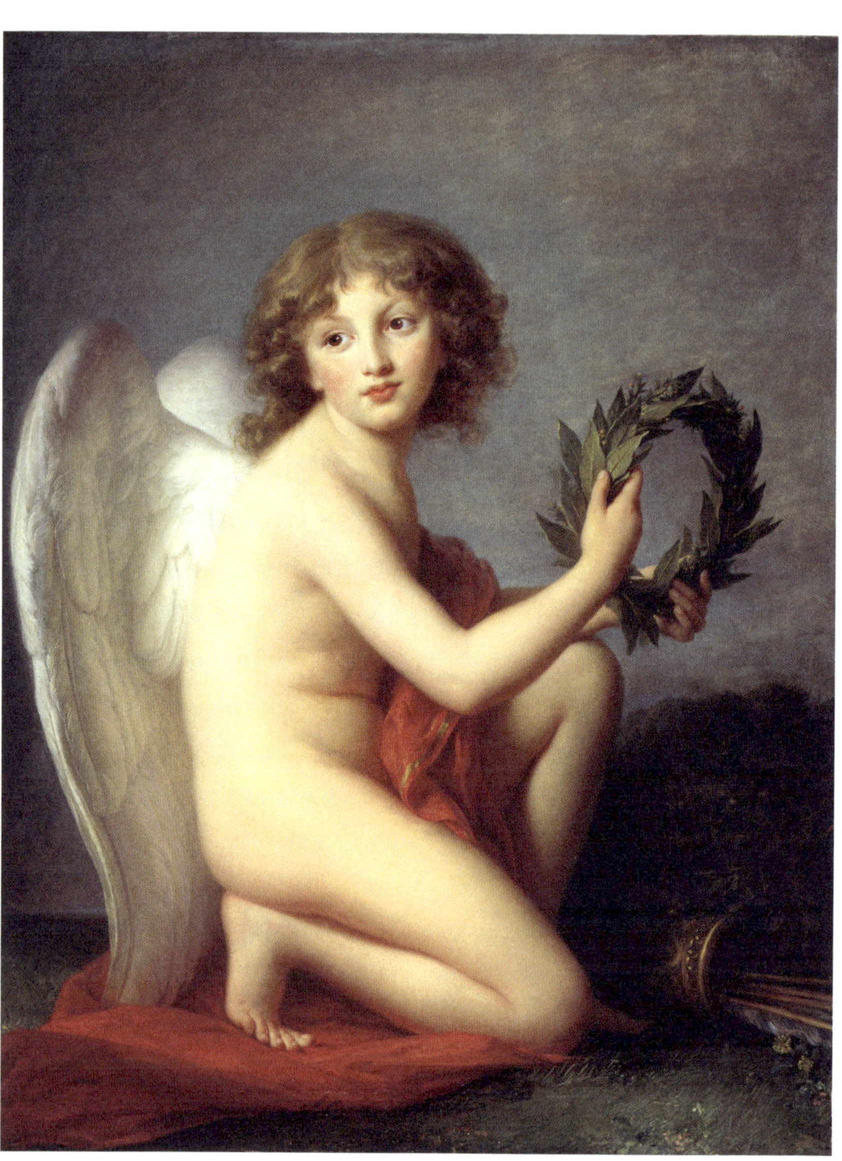

of Naples, Russia, and Prussia, as well as other dignitaries. Born in 1755 to a painter and a hairdresser, Vigée-Lebrun achieved success in France and Europe against the norms of the time during one of the most turbulent periods in European history. Her father, who recognized the daughter's talent and passion early on, died when she was twelve. In her feminist essay "Why Have There Been No Great Women Artists?" from 1971, the art historian Linda Nochlin noted that, denied access to workshops, academies, or universities, almost all women artists known to us before the twentieth century had a father in the profession.[1]

From around 2,800 paintings in the Gemäldegalerie's collection made north and south of the Alps between the thirteenth and the eighteenth century, fifteen were painted by nine women. With the exception of Italian Renaissance painter Sofonisba Anguissola, all of them came from the northern countries and lived around the eighteenth century.[2]

Vigée-Lebrun learned to paint by looking at and copying art in Paris, and began working as a portraitist in her youth, supporting her widowed mother and brother for a time. Soon after encountering Marie Antoinette, she became her court painter, the first woman to attain this rank. Admitted to the Académie Royale de Peinture et de Sculpture (Royal Academy of Painting and Sculpture) at age twenty-eight, she became one of only four women members and one of the leading portraitists of the *ancien régime*.

Neither boy nor girl, neither adult nor child; not completely human, animal, or divine, the prince holds a laurel wreath demonstratively in the air. It is an opening waiting to be breached, whereas the phallic quiver of arrows laying partially concealed at his feet is a latent weapon, a possible complement to entering the ring. Echoing this potential intercourse or coupling, the prince's winged figure hybridizes classic mythology with Jewish-Christian motifs. Cupid-Eros—the mischievous god of love equipped here with arrows but no bow,

1 Linda Nochlin, "Why Have There Been No Great Women Artists?" *ARTnews* (January 1971), p. 22.
2 They are Anne Vallayer-Coster, Marie-Eléonore Godefroid, Anne Geneviève Greuze, Angelica Kauffmann, Judith Leyster, und Rachel Ruysch, Anna Dorothea Therbusch, and Élisabeth Vigée-Lebrun.

a reminder of the ancient knot that ties love with a wound—is combined with a Judeo-Christian angel: a cherub or seraph. The two cherubim in rabbinic literature are described as human-like entities with wings, placed on the opposite ends of the Ark of the Covenant in the inner sanctum of the temple, containing the two stone tablets of the Ten Commandments. Representing a threshold between profane and sacred, between the given world and the one beyond, they guard the law. Higher in ancient Judism and Christianity's hierarchy of angels, the seraphim announce the sacred name of God and its distinction from its creations. These winged creatures separate and connect human and divine, man and God.

In Western iconography, the distinction between seraph and cherub echoes the broad division between faith and reason; cherubs, the former; seraphs, the latter. Cupid as cherub thus takes the pagan idea of a demigod and superimposes it on the Catholic notion of an angel of the sort linked with encouragement to faith as opposed to reason; the latter would be the seraph's concern. The hybridization of Cupid and cherub may therefore point to an aspiration of synthesizing desire and faith. Could it be that the little prince's androgyny, with the ambiguities or thresholds it captures, reverberates the zeitgeist of drastic transformations? The revolutionary program of the period was marked by—or part of—a secularization of the divine, the exchange of the metaphysics of religion with revolutionary ideas and the loss of the sacred. What exactly was Vigée-Lebrun idolizing in her Lubomirski portrait?

The genius of love, disguised in a portrait of a boy, not only evokes a sense of immanentization (as Greco-Roman gods often do, anthropomorphized and restlessly intervening in human affairs) but also implies a certain diffusion or inversion within the active/passive oppositions of man and woman, artist and model, subject and object. As a portraitist at a time when women were denied apprenticeships and forbidden from drawing nudes, Vigée-Lebrun was aware of the power relations inherent to the gaze. In her memoir, she admits to flirting with her male sitters: "As soon as I observed any intention on their part of making sheep's eyes at me, I would paint them looking in another direction than mine, and then, at the least movement of the pupilla, would say, I am doing the eyes now."[3]

Even when women were already officially permitted at the School of Fine Arts in Paris (and in other European art schools) much later at the end of the nineteenth century, they were still not allowed to copy the naked body. That undressed, to-be-painted body was not only standing for painting itself and the speculation of a passivity/activity dichotomy, but also to the question of truth, the naked truth. That was the time when Friedrich Nietzsche stressed how much the questions of art, style, and truth can not be dissociated from the question of the woman.[4] An answer to the question "what is woman" cannot be found in any of the familiar modes of concept or knowledge, he noted. Yet it is impossible to resist looking for her. Men, asserts French philosopher Geneviève Fraisse, didn't want women involved in the question of beauty, because it is married to the question of truth.[5] It belonged to men. Copying the naked body, therefore, is also about gaining access to the truth.

Is there a difference between feminine and masculine creativity? And if there is one, how is it to be argued? Nochlin's essay laid ground for a feminist methodology in art history, claiming that this question was the wrong one to begin with. Acknowledging that "there *were* no women equivalents for Michelangelo or Rembrandt, Cézanne, Picasso or Matisse, or even for de Kooning or Warhol," she made the point that the fault lay not in women's genetics, but rather in institutions and education. As well as that art is not a means of pure self-expression but rather something that involves a self-consistent language of form, given conventions, which must be learned through teaching or individual work. Women were consistently and systematically denied access to both. In addition, she criticized the myth of the innate genius as an atemporal and mysterious power, embedded in the person of the great artist, a godlike figure.

Darren Aronofsky's allegorical film *Mother!* (2017) is dedicated to such figures. It tells the story of a middle-aged poet played by Javier Bardem and his younger partner (Jennifer Lawrence), who are

3 See Élisabeth Vigée-Lebrun, *The Memoirs of Madame Vigée-Lebrun*, trans. Lionel Strachey (New York, 1903).
4 Jacques Derrida, *Spurs: Nietzsche's Styles*, trans. Barbara Harlow (Venice, 1976), p. 59.
5 Interview with Geneviève Fraisse, *The Right to Truth, Conversations on Art and Feminism* (Paris, 2017).

renovating the large remote house in which they live. The house had been demolished by fire and the woman wishes to bring life back into it. While the poet suffers from writer's block, she wants to create a paradise for the two of them with immense contemplation, grace, and craft. Then, in the second part of the film, the woman is pregnant and the man starts writing again. His book becomes a big success at exactly the point that her pregnancy is nearly at term, and, when fans arrive at their house while she's in labor, horrific trouble occurs.

Imbued with biblical symbolism, *Mother!* avails the drama of personal relationship, which is an artistic allegory of masculine and feminine modes of creativity. The characters' namelessness emphasizes this. The writer embodies a godlike principle of creation, with its essential soulless void: a drive derived from a bottomless need for public acknowledgment and worship that turns monstrous. The woman (mother) serves as the sole point of view throughout the film, whose story is told through three types of handheld shots that follow Lawrence around the house as if the camera were physically connected to her: Close-ups zoom in on her face; over-the-shoulder and point-of-view shots show what she sees. She gives life and redemption, first to the house and then to a child. He is creative; she is fertile. She sees; he is blind. He is entitled; she is devoted. Their story unfolds between sterility and fertility, artistic creation and procreation. He is a god of creation; she is a goddess of grace. But while she thinks the house is hers, her hyperventilation—manifested by extreme, swirling close-ups and a voice that sounds both internal and external—merges with the organism of the house: it bleeds and leaks, cracks and threatens her, it is in fact the domain of the man, and finally will turn against her. She is merely a passing inhabitant, between destruction and construction.

The Lubomirski portrait was commissioned by the Polish princess for the fee of 12,000 francs (the equivalent of about 8,500 euros today). Vigée-Lebrun, who was known for the high prices of her paintings enabling her to support herself, was however obliged to give this sum to her husband Jean Baptiste Pierre Lebrun, who was a Parisian art dealer, critic, and inveterate gambler ("I begged M. Lebrun to let me keep forty; but he would not let me have even that").[6] Focusing on portraiture, a painterly genre ranked well below history painting in the eighteenth century and just slightly above still life, Vigée-Lebrun was adhering to her talent or being pragmatic, or both. Either way, painting portraits enabled her to improve her social status, while also committing to its feminine aspects: being of service, deploying empathy, and making use of social skills.

Two self-portraits of Vigée-Lebrun from the seventeen-eighties, however—once as Rubens's beloved second wife Helena Fourment and the other as *La Fornarina* (the young baker) featuring most probably Margherita Luti, Raphael's Roman lover—show that by staging herself in identification with an image (the female lovers) she also perceived herself and wished to be accepted in continuity with the great male painters themselves, and even indirectly challenge them. While Nochlin and much of feminist art history after her rightly stressed the importance of the institutional over the individual, the question that is asked too little today is not whether women can make art or not anymore, but if and how women can be creative without adopting masculine attributes, without being creative like a man. Does the fact that there is no *female style* in the works of great women artists from Artemesia Gentileschi to Agnes Martin mean that there's nothing in common among women artists? Can a woman artist define art anew in radicality like, for example, Diego Velázquez, Marcel Duchamp, or Andy Warhol, or is it a different game altogether? Can the creativity of women extricate itself from the metaphor, from being an image; one that belongs to the sphere of mere appearances and temptation, but also to nature and motherhood?

Between its two facets—the monstrous imagination of an endless birth-giving, as opposed to a suffering of being as endurance, in absence—what are the paradoxes within which art is made by women? Corresponding to the former is much of performance art by women since the nineteen-seventies, which relates to taboo aspects of bodies: menstrual blood, childbearing, excrement, internal organs; or, differently, art made by and after Louise Bourgeois's Surrealism, vividly feeding off trauma and lending unconscious visual tropes

6 "My indifference to money no doubt proceeded from the fact that wealth was not necessary to me. Since that which made my house pleasant required no extravagance, I always lived very economically. I spent very little on dress; I was even reproached for neglecting it, for I wore none but white dresses of muslin or lawn, and never wore elaborate gowns excepting for my sittings at Versailles. My head-dress cost me nothing, because I did my hair myself, and most of the time I wore a muslin cap on my head, as may be seen from my portraits." Vigée-Lebrun 1903 (see note 3).

(stairs, spiders, cages) meaning that is both narrative and therapeutic. In correlation to the latter, one can think of Agnes Martin's repetitive grids that achieve "not what is seen, but what is known forever in the mind" unfolding contemplative states of existence. Or Vija Celmins's detailed drawings and paintings of starry skies, spider webs, or the ocean as surfaces of spiritual solitude and retinal allure.

"Pregnancy has made females gentler, more expectant, more timid, more submissively inclined; and similarly, intellectual pregnancy engenders the character of the contemplative, who are allied to women in character—they are the masculine mothers," Nietzsche writes, referring to his thoughts like a woman speaking of her child.[7] Rooted in antiquity, the concept of the genius artist reached a powerful form in the eighteenth and nineteenth centuries, with a noteworthy paradox. While it explicitly excluded women artists, womanly metaphors of conception, gestation, labor, and birth were employed in describing artistic creativity.[8] Actual childbirth, in contrast, was regarded as part of woman's natural role, and her own emotions and sensitivities were thought as mere manifestations of nature's gift.

While the genius of the male artist produced new creations that transcend the dictates of nature, her artistic expression was designated less an achievement and more a natural display, a byproduct. Aronofsky, who cast Lawrence, his lover at the time, to navigate his allegory of the artistic act in *Mother!*—reaching his own life and filming process—exposed the depth of these intertwined categories and how much they still activate our imagination and thinking. Simply turning the divisions on their heads will not suffice to comprehend the differences between masculine and feminine creativity. Resisting *passivity* results merely in women aspiring to be men.

If the domain of modern art and artifice is understood as a substitute for fecundity, an outcome of a creativity which is in its essence masculine, what art can be made in fertility? Asking this question might risk all that women's fight for equality has accomplished. However, not asking it might be denying the potentialities of art made by women as something that can best be described as total otherness in this given, androcentric world.

7 Friedrich Nietzsche, *The Joyful Wisdom*, trans. Thomas Common (Edinburgh and London, 1910).
8 See Christine Battersby, *Gender and Genius: Towards a Feminist Aesthetics* (Bloomington, 1989).

The Vertigo of Time

Étienne Chevalier with St. Stephen and *Madonna Surrounded by Seraphim and Cherubim*, also known as *The Melun Diptych* (ca. 1455) by Jean Fouquet

The Madonna glows. The picture is wholly artificial in its square format, spatial flatness, and dominant geometric shapes, most prominently a spherical stone-white breast, uncovered and protruding as though there were no gravity in the space where this celestial breastfeeding takes place. There are unnatural, predominating *Le Tricolore* reds, whites, and blues—at the time already associated with the reigning houses of France—and fabrics that look as if they were carved in marble, including the Madonna's cotehardie dress. A troupe of cherubim and seraphim in dark red and indigo blue, seemingly molded out of a synthetic material, frame the Madonna, interwoven with each other into a pattern that completely fills the ground.

Despite its appearance, this painting is also strangely vibrant. While the angels, a transparent veil, throne, and a crown of pearls and rubies indicate the holiness of a heavenly queen, the Madonna also radiates human eroticism and humility. While baby Jesus's face is frozen and his body icily suspended, the angels' monochrome faces, each turning its gaze in a different direction, surround mother and child with a web of looks, including one directly at the viewer, and are animated with human expressions.

This shining square painting on oak is the right panel of *The Melun Diptych*, made by Jean Fouquet around 1455. The *Madonna lactans*—Mother Mary nursing infant Jesus—is frontally placed while the baby directs his gaze to the diptych's left panel, connecting the two parts. There, Étienne Chevalier, treasurer to the French monarchs Charles VII and Louis XI and the work's benefactor, is depicted kneeling in front of the holy mother and child in the right panel. He is escorted by his guardian patron Saint Stephen (Étienne) whose half-profile exposes his freshly wounded tonsure-shaved head, bleeding thick

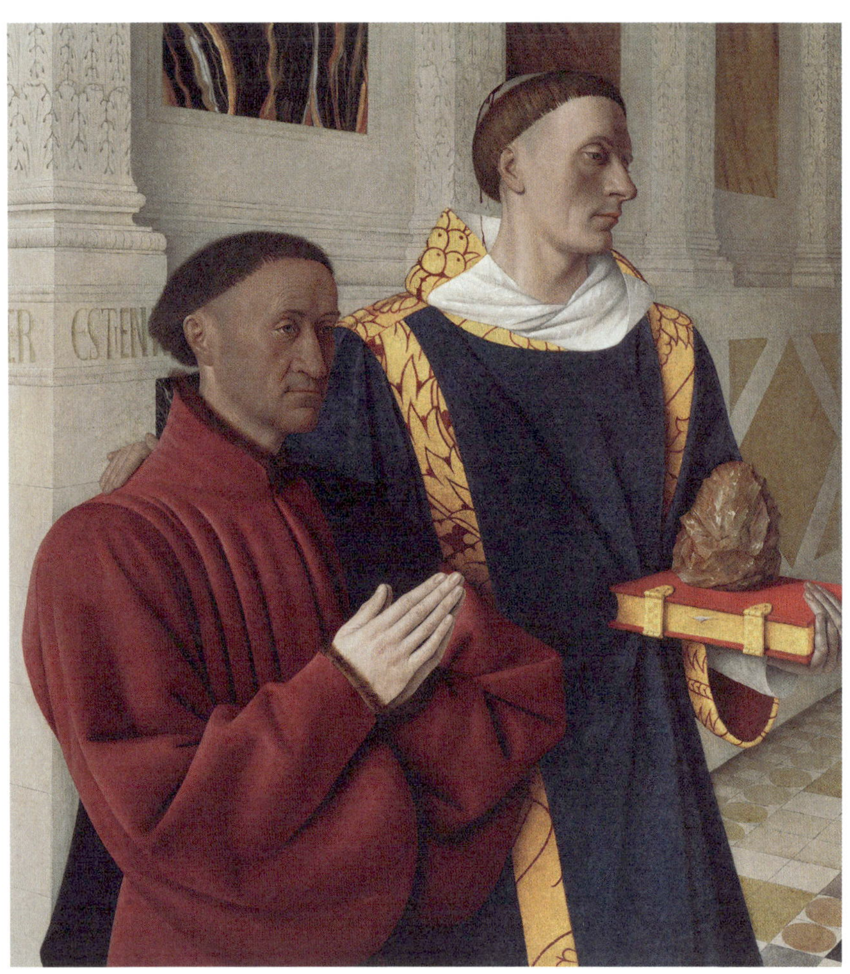

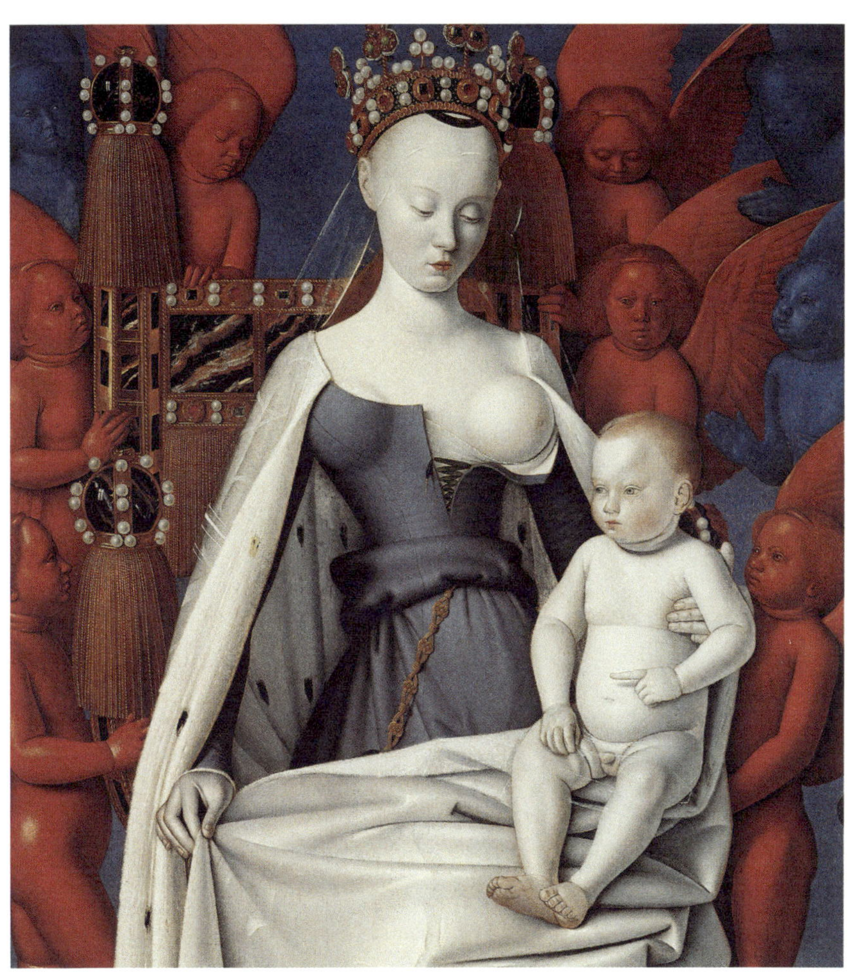

red drops that fall into the red pattern on the brocade gold braid of his blue dalmatic. The serrated stone that the protomartyr holds corresponds to his martyrdom—he was stoned to death in Jerusalem—but also reverberates with the child's head in the opposite panel, whose gaze is directed precisely at Stephen's stone. This rock, assembling the baby's and our attention at the center of the diptych, is more natural-looking and warmer in color than the infant's marble-like head and body. It may as well be a meteor fallen from heaven to sit upon Saint Stephen's scripture, anticipating (the baby's) past and future; death and resurrection.

Étienne Chevalier from Melun was one of Jean Fouquet's primary patrons, who commissioned the work for the tomb of his wife Catherine Budé, who died an untimely death. It was to be placed in the couple's mausoleum (Chevalier would follow his wife twenty-two years later) at the Notre Dame cathedral in Melun southeast of Paris. The diptych was probably an altarpiece with one wing fixed to a wall, while the other wing could be opened and closed like a book and was likely painted on both sides. Meant to demonstrate the patron's political power in a sacred context, all adults are shown in half-length and almost life-size in both panels of the diptych, each almost one meter high, an unprecedented format resulting in a monumental effect. Both Fouquet and Chevalier were in the king's closest circle, participating in and profiting from the shaping of an emerging national identity after the unification of France and the foundation of a monarchy, an outcome of the recent Hundred Years' War. The large scale introduced in this diptych historically followed the miniature. The epic oversize dimension, like the devotional undersize one, resulted in a similar effect of wonder and awe. Fouquet later created for Chevalier a *Book of Hours* (1450–60) with many miniatures, including a diptych with a *Madonnas lactans* and the two Étiennes, the donor and his saint, similarly bowing.

In 1773, each panel of the diptych from the Notre Dame cathedral in Melun was sold separately to finance the building's renovation. The versatile, ostentatious object was thus dissected and partly destroyed—the third image on the back of the left panel is now lost—to become two distinct pictures. The right panel was purchased by the mayor of Antwerp and today belongs to the Koninklijk Museum voor Schone Kunsten (Royal Museum of Fine Arts) there. The left panel was purchased by the Gemäldegalerie in 1896 from the collection of Ludwig Brentano in Frankfurt am Main. The two panels were exhibited together, for the third time since their separation, in the winter of 2017–18 in Berlin. Eighty years prior, in 1937, the diptych was notably shown in Paris at the *Exposition Internationale*, a World Fair overshadowed by hefty political tensions. Germany was assisting the Spanish General Francisco Franco in his war against the democratically elected government of the Second Spanish Republic, using this war as a test run for its *Luftwaffe*, bombing the town of Guernica on April 26, 1937. In the fall of that year, Spain's representation in the fair was Pablo Picasso's seminal painting *Guernica* (1937).

Albert Speer planned the German pavilion with an exaggerated tower crowned with a Nazi eagle and a swastika, which was well received by the public, especially in comparison to the equally monumental Soviet pavilion standing directly across the wide avenue. As the host country, France was seeking to express its modernity by displaying the continuity of French painting in which Fouquet's diptych was chosen to mark a starting point, a rediscovered national emblem. The German Reichskulturkammer (the Third Reich's Chamber of Culture) thus lent the *Melun Diptych*'s left panel to France for the exhibition at the newly built Palais de Tokyo, barely three years before Germany was to conquer the country.

Behind the benefactor and his patron in the left panel, an architectural marble interior opens into the depth, using central perspective to offset the tight, relief-like (Gothic) flat space of the facing right panel and showing what Fouquet must have learned in Italy. Colored marble panels appear between the pilasters in the background on the left, and again in the Madonna's throne to the right. Reds and blues that dominate the Madonna's image appear in the clothing of the donor and his patron, while the grays and whites in the donor's panel can be seen in somewhat cooler hues in the skin of the Madonna and child. The Madonna's iconography belongs to northern European tradition, as do the brittle, incisive lines characteristic of miniature painting flourishing in France, Flanders, and England in manuscripts and devotional books of hours. The use of foreshortening and bodies' volumes show Fouquet's acquaintance with early Renaissance works by Masaccio, Fra Angelico, or Piero della Francesca.

Of the sixteen medallions decorating *The Melun Diptych*'s original frame in blue velvet and golden lace with pearls, now completely lost, only two survived. One in Berlin was probably stolen in 1945; the other is on view at the Louvre in Paris. It is made of painted copper and features a self-portrait of the French painter Jean Fouquet. This is the first independent self-portrait, not composed as part of a scene, made by an artist north of the Alps. Drawn in gold on the dark shiny background, the painter's face directs his sober gaze straight at the viewer. Showing self-assurance next to his signature, he claims what we now call authorship. This may be the first move in a slow transition that artists' self-depictions would undergo—from a signature, like the insertion of the artist's face into his own picture; to an artistic reflection, a means of expressing a subjectivity or at least of presenting a mask thereof.

Fouquet was born in Tours around 1420 and was known in France as *le peintre*, but the successful workshop he supervised in Tours produced many manuscripts and miniatures in addition to paintings. He worked for King Charles VII and was appointed court painter under his successor King Louis XI. A lost portrait of Pope Eugene IV, and a laudatory comment written by the Florentine artist Filarete, tell us he visited Rome in the late 1440s. Early-Renaissance Rome had taught him the theory of central perspective and scale, but little is certain as to how he gained knowledge of Netherlandish art, which affected the way he described materials and surfaces in painting and his elaborate play with light and shadows. Fouquet died in 1480, aged about sixty years.

In the diptych, southern and northern art, depth and flatness, naturalism and geometrical abstraction, meticulously described objects and pure forms are distributed in a sophisticated plan. Gazes cross each other in the air, but never meet, connecting the two panels. The Madonna's introverted gaze is turned down toward the infant, the infant's is directed at the saint's stone; the saint aims his gaze at the infant and the donor directs his gaze forward and outside the picture. But all gazes are spun together by the artist to form a unified space whose vanishing point lies exactly under the Madonna's chin. If the donor's wing were indeed displayed at ninety degrees to the Madonna's, it would create an almost three-dimensional nexus of sight lines enveloping the Madonna like a spider's web and centering around the infant's gaze at the rock, the main component connecting the left and right panels.

The dual scheme of a diptych always involves a tension between unity and polarity. Corresponding to contemporary conventions, it displays a fusion that does not resolve the differences between a secular world and a sacred realm, or between external worlds of sight and vision and inner worlds of insight, imagination, and delirium. On the glossy surface of two colored-marble balls in the throne is a reflection of a window across the room (recalling Flemish painting, especially Jan van Eyck) indicating a closed, darker room, perhaps of an inner life. The interior on the other side is bright and open. Finally, this comprehensive duality also corresponds to the artist's geographical finding between the low countries and Italy, and his historical moment, on the threshold between medieval Europe and the beginning of a modern age.

Toggling between the political and the spiritual, and between the monumental and the devotional, many of the tensions in the diptych are conventional. Yet some seem unusual or radical, even to viewers today. The Queen of Heaven, an almost extraterrestrial apparition in the painting, is at the same time uncannily erotic and atypically fashionable. Her blue garment emphasizes an extremely slight waist; its half-unraveled corset—the edge of the green lace sloping downward as if just untangled—exposes her snow-white skin while an ermine robe rests elegantly on her shoulders.

The woman most likely cast as the Madonna was Agnès Sorel, who would have been dead for at least two years when *The Melun Diptych* was painted. She was considered the most beautiful woman in France, and perhaps the entire world. *La belle Agnès* was the assertive, extroverted mistress of Charles VII and the first woman to be officially recognized as such and granted ruling privileges. This powerful figure, known for her extravagance[1] but also intelligence and sensitivity, was tolerated by the queen Marie d'Anjou, the mother of the king's fourteen children, perhaps with no other choice. Sorel obviously earned many enemies. She died abruptly at the age of twenty-eight, in the fifth year of her relationship with the king and pregnant with their fourth child. Suspicion surrounding the events was so pervasive that in 2005, Sorel's body was exhumed. Forensic scientists determined she had been poisoned. Prior to her death Fouquet had met and portrayed her when she was traveling with the king to Tours. In his Melun painting, he almost literally visualizes the epitaph on her grave that says she was whiter than a swan and redder than a flame.

For the widower Étienne Chevalier, the dead Sorel as Madonna (commemorating his wife, peculiar as it may seem to us) was an homage not only to her, whose testament he was executing, but also for the bereaved king. The morphing of the mistress's image to the Queen of Heaven was not an unprecedented topos in art and in fact reveals a telling split in French culture of contradicting forces: religious faith and worldly splendor. The Madonna bears all resemblance, human beauty, and attractiveness to the dead woman, yet her head and breasts, the core of our gaze, are compass-round (bringing to mind the work of Paolo Uccello and Piero della Francesca), theorizing and neutralizing sensuality. She does not offer her breast to the infant, who does not seem to notice as there is hardly a motherly touch or signs of affection. In his diptych, Fouquet thus gives expression to a culture equally dominated by Christian spirituality and the admiration of, at times even submission to, sensual luxury and excessive creativity residing side by side in the French royal court.

In the eighteenth century, however, the Melun Madonna was considered an ugly depiction of a controversial woman and was displayed in a humble, almost hidden place in the Antwerp museum's galleries. Bare women's breasts have held contradictory potentialities since they appeared in Greek art in the fourth century BC almost simultaneously in the Venus pudica (a modest Venus concealing her genitals) and a single-breasted Amazon (the warrior who cut off one breast to draw a bow). The *Madonna lactans*, too, was a contentious,

1 A dignitary visiting the French court in 1447 complained that Sorel was exposing her nipples, evoking rumors and murmurs; Sorel's fashion choices are documented as an ongoing scandal.

controversial theme in European art after the Renaissance, treading the line between the sexual, the maternal, and the pious. Later in France, national symbols Joan of Arc and Marianne, the revolutionary personification of liberty, would be recognized by their breasts; one covered with a military breastplate and the other exposed in battle.

But what if this thread of deceased women, connected to each other and reflected in each other, reveals that something else is at play? What does the incorporation of Mary, the spiritual queen and breastfeeding virgin; Sorel, the poisoned, sensual, pregnant lover; and Budé, the late wife of a powerful man and the mother of his three children (not depicted but implied) all in one figure tell us? Perhaps this icy queen, this marble-skinned figure, artificial and painfully real at once, painted when her model was already dead with an unborn child, embodies a metaphysical wound, as the saint's bleeding head may indicate.

The infant held at a distance and seated on the rigid fabric will eventually be resurrected after his death. He provides evidence to the complicity of his very image, and in fact every image, with the desire to halt time. It is said that death will be swallowed and defeated "when the perishable has been clothed with the imperishable, and the mortal with immortality. Death, where is your victory?" Paul writes in the Corinthians. Can one conquer death by imagining the face of a dead woman? If she is carefully represented, perhaps she is not dead. Her depiction is what the kneeling benefactor looks at, or dreams of—if the division of panels splits a world and its reflection, the attempt to resurrect love is also an attempt to refute time. Fouquet's Mary-Agnès-Catherine is an object-painting working against time's passage which both denies and accepts its corrosion. Like Orpheus's song, it pulls Eurydice out of the Sheol, only to put her to death again, irreversibly, with his gaze.

The Architecture of Heaven

The Madonna in the Church (ca. 1440) by Jan van Eyck

This small, vertically oriented painting leads us through an arched window into an opulent cathedral nave, enclosing a Madonna and child. Pouring in from a row of upper windows, warm light floods the figures of Mary and her baby and is thrown back at us almost like a small torch. But it is easy to miss the painting in the gallery. *The Madonna in a Church* measures just thirty-one by twenty-four centimeters, and is hung behind glass in a vitrine. Difficult to comprehend and somewhat hypnotizing is how this entire miraculous and hyper-realistic space is compressed into a rectangle only slightly larger than a postcard.

The Madonna's childlike face is tilted elegantly; a large crown, decorated with royal blue and red gemstones, is laid heavily upon her head. The baby grabs her glittering necklace, which echoes the crown in its design, as real babies do. Jewels, indicating holiness in the first half of the fifteenth century, were shown in paintings, often with gold leaves or pastiched gemstones. In his endeavor to pin down the effects of holiness in art, the German theologian Rudolf Otto stressed how much the magical impression that buildings, decorations, or artifacts seek to nurture and serve to localize, accumulate, and connect to the numinous. In the Gothic cathedral, for example, the numinous is addressed with artistic means of the sublime.[1]

But van Eyck used only one material, oil paint, to create surfaces consistent in themselves and in continuity with our world. The sacredness that van Eyck's viewers may have expected to find

1 The "numinous" is a notion Otto elaborated upon in his writings to stand for a holiness independent of the ethics linked to it over time in many cultures. The numinous represents the powerful effects of the divine in human experience. See Rudolf Otto, *Das Heilige* (Munich, 2013), p. 85.

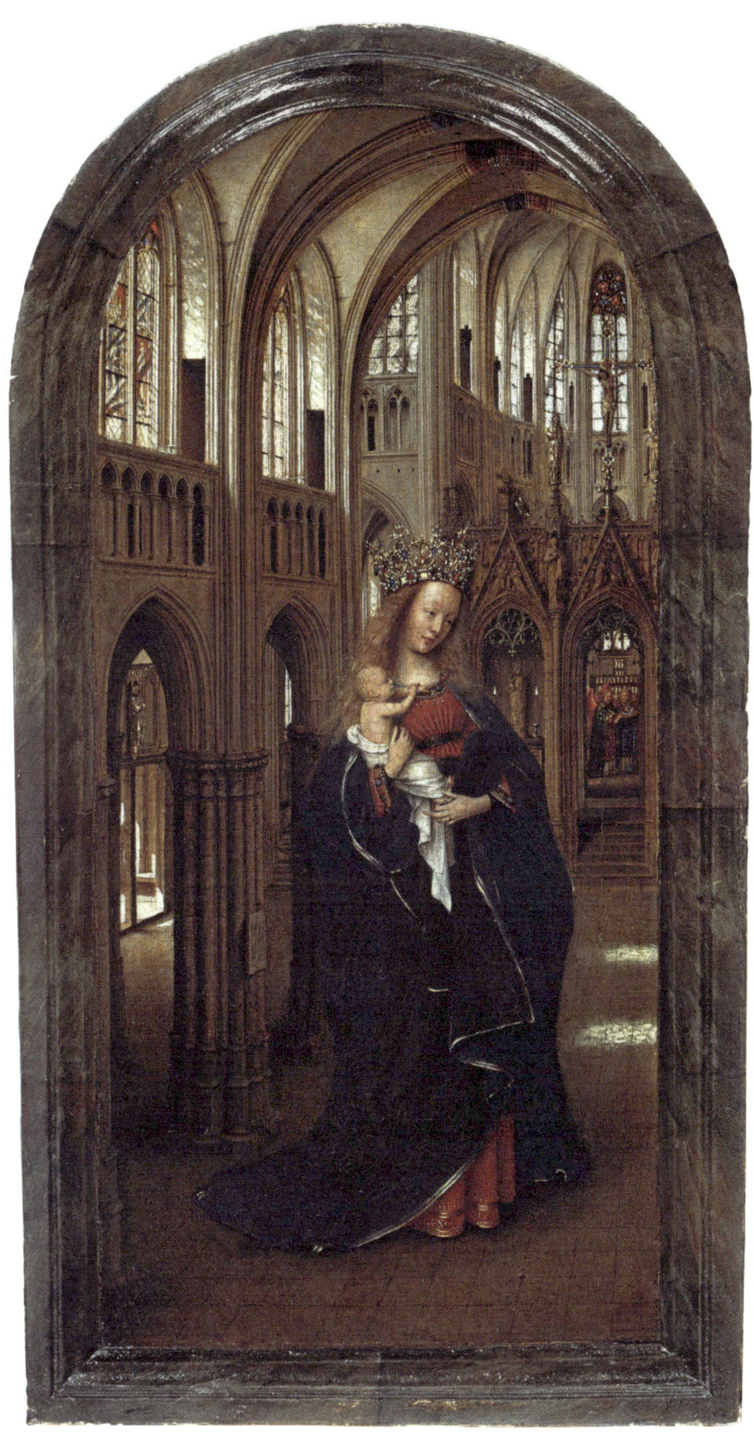

in paintings—bringing them into closer physical contact with the objects of their faith, entering their souls by means of sight—is brought down to earth with meticulous precision in his hands. There is no differentiation in resolution or focus. All details are painted with similar accuracy. For the viewer, the illusion of these paintings, the fiction of the painted world as real, never breaks.

Surprisingly, the relatively large figure of the Madonna—her crowned head reaches the level of the cathedral's triforium—does not decrease the effect of the spacious interior behind her. In fact, the diagonal view, placing us inside the church while light enters through the side porch and windows on the left, all make the church look enormous. The picture's frame crops the dome at the choir's top, emphasizing, too, that its height goes beyond the painting's limits. The Madonna's scale, disproportionate in comparison to the naturalistically depicted baby and more extremely with the building that surrounds her, has perplexed modern viewers and raised art historians' eyebrows. Yet viewers in van Eyck's time might not even have noticed it or thought it to be awkward.

With the introduction of perspective to pictures, in a world at the threshold of the modern age, painting, such as van Eyck's and his environment, committed itself more and more to naturalism. It implied that if the surface of the painting were understood as a window through which we look, the same rules should apply to the pictorial space as to the empirical one. Yet this new naturalism had to be reconciled with more than a thousand years of Christian tradition, Erwin Panofsky wrote, discussing van Eyck's art. A non-naturalistic art that does not recognize unity of space or time can employ symbols without regard for empirical probability. The unrealistic size of the Madonna in the church can therefore be conceived as a resolution for this significant ambivalence. A symbolism that is concealed in the truthful appearance of things, Panofsky called it "disguised symbolism."[2] More than a woman, mother, or even queen, the Madonna appears to be supernatural. Either corresponding to or contradicting this, she may stand for an idea and an institution: the *ecclesia* (the community of believers), heavenly and human-made. The frame of

2 Erwin Panofsky, *Early Netherlandish Painting* (Cambridge, MA, 1966), p.141.

this painting, too, belongs to both the new and old worlds.[3] Probably the left wing of a diptych whose other half is long lost, the frame simulates a window through which we look at the projected imaginary space. Yet it is part of the painting, adjusted in color as an imitation of marble, indicating the painting being a tangible artifact and stressing its materiality. If paintings were beautiful things prior to van Eyck, his paintings are both precious objects and worlds opening in front of us; worlds in which we find ourselves included.

Apart from some forty archival documents and twenty artworks, little is known about Jan van Eyck's life even though his paintings include signature dates and self-portraits. Born around 1390 in Maaseik near Maastricht, in 1425 he became the court painter of the Duke of Burgundy in Lille, whose lands in the fifteenth century reached to Flanders. In his relentless rivalry with other courts, the Duke, known as Philip the Good, was a vigorous force in northern Europe in turning painting and sculpture to superior arts, replacing finely crafted luxury objects like jewelry or wall tapestries that until then served as major currency and symbols of dominance and capital. Jan van Eyck was close to the powerful man, and a portrait he made of Isabella of Portugal in a secret mission to search for potential spouses on behalf of the Duke resulted in their marriage. The Duke converted the artist's annual salary to a lifelong pension, telling the reluctant bookkeepers that "we would not find another so much to our liking, nor so excellent in his art and science."

In addition to his function as a court artist, van Eyck executed private commissions. Such was the case with complex polyptych altarpiece for a private chapel in Ghent, completed in 1432 with his brother Hubert van Eyck, about whom almost nothing is known. With its human-faced lamb, recently sensationally discovered as part of a comprehensive restoration, the Ghent Altarpiece is considered to have launched an image revolution, alongside a double portrait from ca. 1434 now known as *The Arnolfini Wedding* (in which neither the name Arnolfini nor a wedding is a certain fact), probably

3 The frame was long thought to have been added to the painting in the nineteenth century. It was recently confirmed that this frame is actually much older and might be the original. See Stephan Kemperdick, "Jan van Eyck's Madonna in a Church and its Artistic Legacy," in *Jan van Eyck, An Optical Revolution*, exh cat. Museum of Fine Arts Ghent (Ghent, 2020).

depicting an Italian merchant in Bruges with his wife. Now hanging in the National Gallery in London, this is likely one of the world's most puzzling paintings in which realism, as it discovers itself—including a painted mirror reflecting the depicted room and perhaps the artist himself—leaves us forever uncertain if what it reveals is merely deception.

In his 1568 edition of *Lives of the Artists*, Giorgio Vasari famously crowned van Eyck as the inventor of oil painting. He ascribed mystical powers and carefully kept secrecy to the Flemish artist and wrote that he took "great delight in alchemy." More significantly, he claimed Italian Renaissance masters were deeply indebted to van Eyck's invention. There was oil painting long before van Eyck, probably since antiquity, but his method was indeed radically new, and it irreversibly influenced painting with its quick drying procedures and easier portability of the panels or canvases, as well as the new possibilities of rendering human skin based on layering paint and glazes for deeper effect. Each color surface reflected light differently, the way the materials that those surfaces represent do; the paint thus took on the character of what it depicted. Rather than making his paintings resemble what he saw, van Eyck seems to have tried to recreate it. Oil paint with van Eyck first revealed itself as an inevitable, necessary instrument, prompting painting to become a distinguished art medium that it remains until today. As with other technological inventions, these innovations were not quite "discoveries," but rather possibilities that were latently there all along, noticed and picked up at a certain moment when conditions and needs were ripe to create a revolution.

The light falling from the left side of the cathedral implies a world outside and a sunny day. Yet if this realistic church is facing east, as all medieval churches and Gothic cathedrals do, light should have entered the building from the other direction. This light has evoked different theories, but one thing remains beyond doubt: as much as this Gothic cathedral is accurately and realistically depicted, it does not refer to an existing building. There are two occurrences in all of Jan van Eyck's paintings in which a specific building—a cathedral tower that looks like the one in Utrecht—can be identified: in the

Ghent Altarpiece and in the landscape viewed from the porch in the *Madonna of Chancellor Rolin* (ca. 1435). Other than that, all paintings tell stories that take place in entirely invented hyperrealistic buildings. These are architectural pastiches that could have been built, but were not. Many painters in the early Renaissance were also architects; paintings served to examine new ideas.[4] But van Eyck, as far as we know, was hardly interested in building himself; he seems as much invested in inventing an architecture that also serves as a metaphor.

If the light from the north is supernatural, the church is more than a building. As opposed to the earthly, the heavenly Jerusalem that will be inhabited after the end of time is not geographically fixed; therefore it was only plausible that it be depicted in the shape of the European cities artists visited or lived in. In the Talmud, the "Jerusalem above" is a worldly city that is also a district of the spirit. For many Christians, the New Jerusalem, coming down from heaven, is the consummation of the Body of Christ, the Church.

John's vision in the Book of Revelations reads: "And there shall be no night there; and they need no candle, neither light of the sun; for the Lord God giveth them light: and they shall reign for ever and ever." Not everyone agrees on this interpretation of the northern light, but on the trim of the Virgin's majestic red robe, we find another reference to divine light. A Latin text embroidered in gold, reads (in translation): "Being compared with the natural light, she is found before it. She is the brightness of eternal light, and the flawless mirror of God's majesty." The Virgin is a perfectly reflected light, with God being the illuminating source.[5]

Light had become an almost autonomous protagonist in van Eyck's mature works (as far as they can be precisely dated); no longer just a vehicle to define materiality and volume of all surfaces by

4 "Without architecture," Italian architect Sebastiano Serlio said, "there is no perspective. Yet without perspective, there is no architecture." See Hubert Damisch, *Noah's Ark* (Cambridge, MA, 2016).

5 "This text is the Little Chapter for Lauds on the Feast of the Assumption according to the use of several Flemish, North French, and Lower Rhenish dioceses. Taken from the Book of Wisdom VII, 29 and 26, it claims that Divine Wisdom as diffused in the Universal Church and embodied in the Virgin Mary is more beautiful than the sun and above the whole order of the stars." Panofsky 1966 (see note 2), p. 148.

means of oil painting, but finally an entity that narrates the painting more than human action. For many years, *The Madonna in a Church* was considered an early work of the Flemish artist, the last painting signed by him is from 1439. But it is precisely the artist's processing of light in this picture that had persuaded historians that this is in fact van Eyck's last painting, completed before his death in the summer of 1441.[6]

Behind the Madonna in the painting, a small sculpted duplication of her can be seen, standing between two burning candles. The grisaille stone not only manifests the old paragone—the debate regarding which art mediums are superior—but also intensifies the lifelike way in which the "real" Madonna (who is, after all also indicated as not real) is painted. Like a lesser God, the artist can create light and life. Van Eyck signed all his works with the motto *Als ich chan* (as best I can), pointing to both omnipotence and acknowledging worldly limits. Like a godly act, his was painting that would hide that it was painted, that it was ever "made," but would simultaneously show off the meticulous human labor invested in it (and indeed van Eyck raised the general prices of painting, due to that fact). It is a declaration of vanity and restraint.

6 Kemperdick 2020 (see note 3).

Zooming In

The Presentation of Christ in the Temple (ca. 1454) by Andrea Mantegna

When Joseph and Mary brought the newborn Jesus to the Jerusalem temple for a consecration to the Lord (or, most likely, circumcision) in the Gospel of Luke, they also brought a pair of doves. The lesser animal sacrifice is not depicted in Andrea Mantegna's dense painterly interpretation of the scene, nor are any other props or details of the temple or altar. Representing this popular religious theme, Mantegna, who was born in 1431 near Padua as a son of a carpenter and died in 1506 in Mantua as an acclaimed but bankrupted court painter for the Gonzaga dynasty, had abandoned previous painters' conventions.

Like anyone living and working in Padua, the northern Italian city of the Venetian Republic, he must have thoroughly known Giotto's fresco of the *The Presentation of Christ in the Temple* (ca. 1303) at the Scrovegni Chapel, which narrates the sacred scene with full-size protagonists in an architectural composition commensurate to the conventions of the time. Yet for his own take from 1454, young Mantegna seems to have been informed much more by the work of Donatello (Donato di Niccolò di Betto Bardi), the Florentine sculptor who had worked in Padua. Mantegna was twelve years old when Donatello arrived, aged almost sixty. In Padua, Donatello, who was the first artist to have taken interest in his friend's invention—Filippo Brunelleschi's mathematical perspective for the representation of space—was to complete the first freestanding equestrian monument since antiquity. No one had cast a horse in bronze since the Romans, as he did with the full size, realistic *Equestrian monument of Erasmo da Narni (Gattamelata)* (1447–53) in Padua's Piazza del Santo. The portrayal of a man astride a true-to-life horse in motion made way for sculpture to liberate itself from the constraints of architecture.

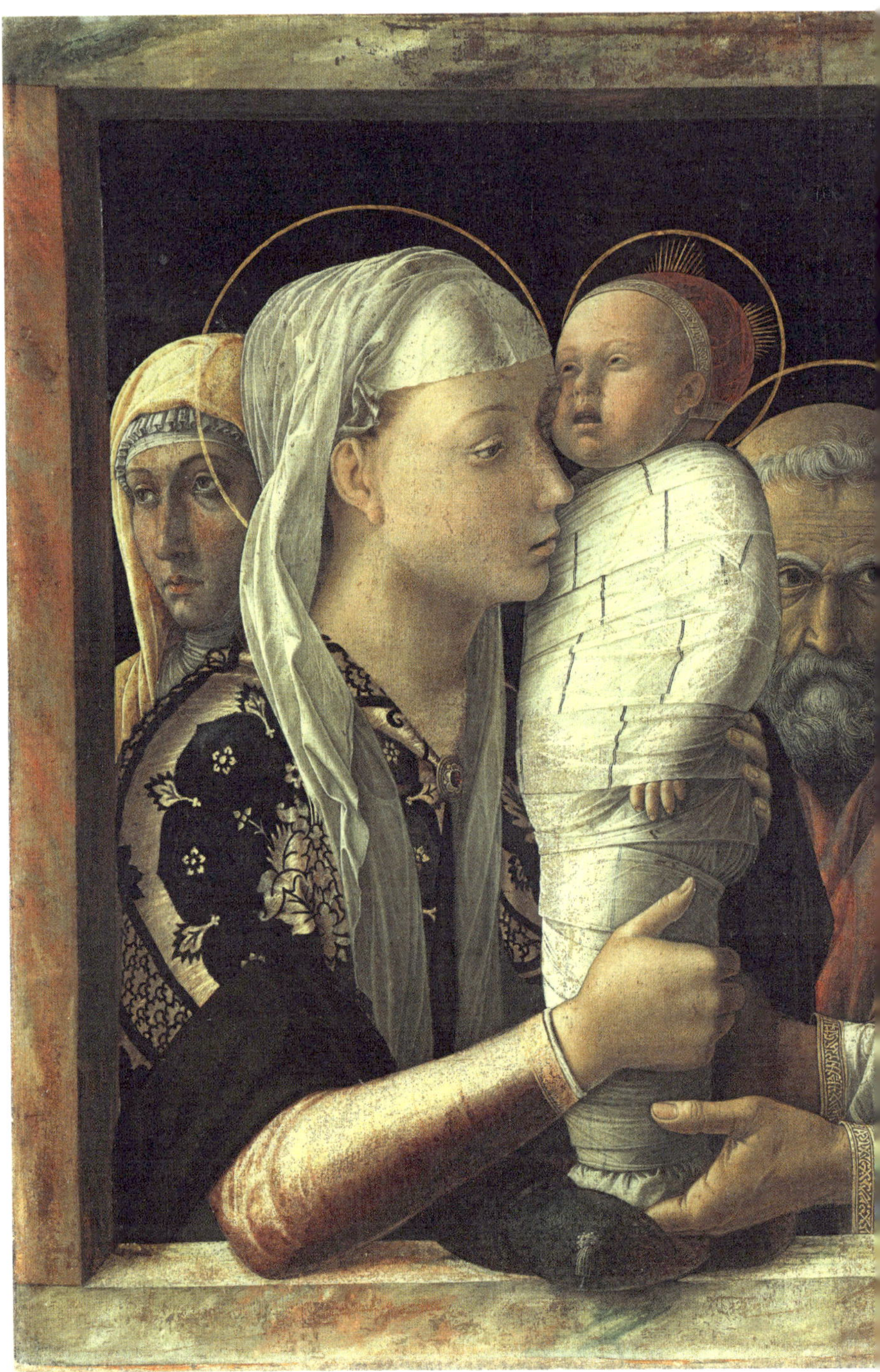

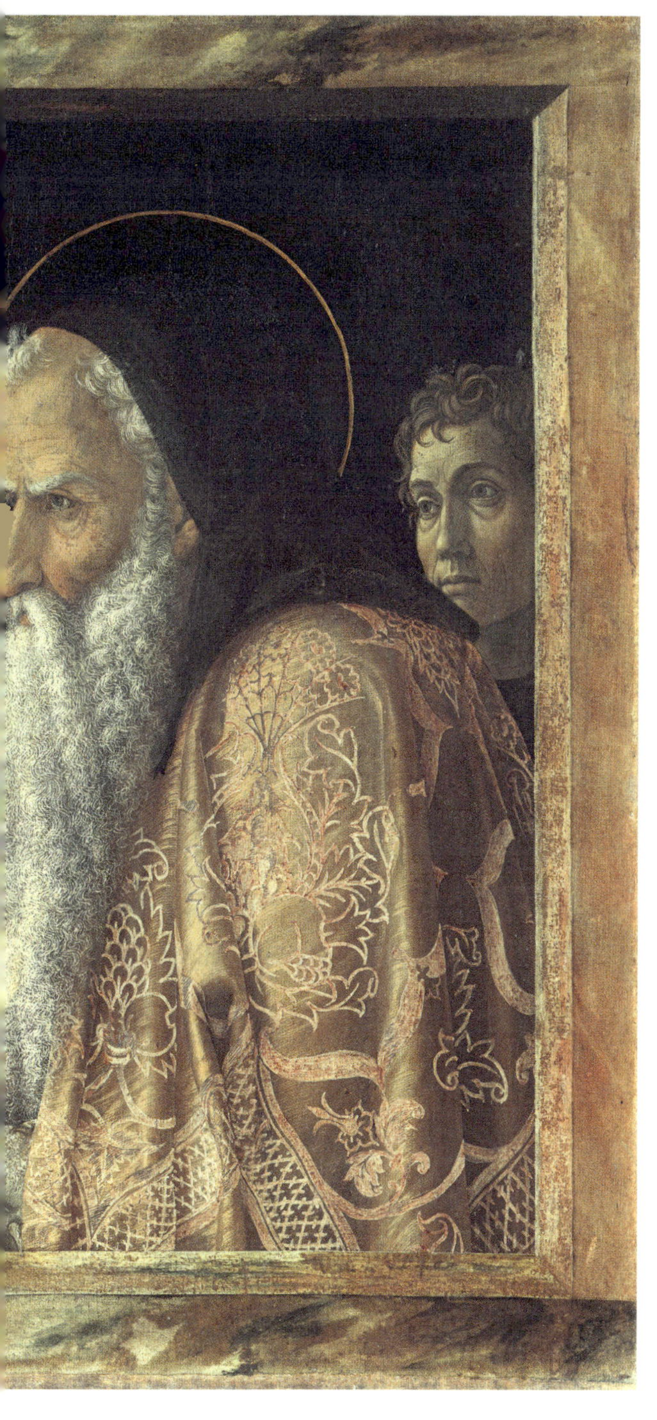

Mantegna was known to be one of the first Renaissance artists who, following Donatello, (re)used verisimilitudinous space perspective with virtuosity. His later painting *The Lamentation of Christ* (1480) in Milan is a captivatingly awkward exaggeration of Renaissance foreshortening. It shows a steep view of the dead Christ foot to head, laid out on a slab of marble, positioning the viewer, who is inevitably moved, at the feet of Christ in the place of Mary Magdalene, who bathed these feet with her tears. But in *The Presentation*, Mantegna cuts his figures at the waist and crowds them together into a space surrounded by a painted marble frame and against a plain dark background, as if zooming into a flat close-up. The group's tight compression makes the picture plane almost two-dimensional, and the figures seem as if they were carved on a frieze.

In the foreground, Simeon, a wise elder with a meticulously depicted long beard—each frizzy white hair delineated with the thin lines of egg-tempera paint—and a solemn bearing, determinately grasps the feet of the baby, whom he recognizes as the Messiah according to the Gospel of Luke. The tenderly represented gesture of the sorrowful mother, the curves of her pale profile perfectly completing the crying baby's cheek like two puzzle pieces, indicates the ambiguity between the fraught obligations of motherhood and an agonizing acknowledgement of the burden her baby will take on, or a rejection thereof.

Unlike Giotto's Mary, she seems to pull the infant away from Simeon with both her arms (in Catholic devotion the prophecy of Simeon is the first of the Seven Sorrows of Mary, even though *The Presentation* belongs to the sequence of the Joyful Mysteries), as if wishing to keep him with her in the human dimension and saving him from his destiny. This almost symbiotic portrayal—an X-ray of the painting shows that Mantegna had later drawn the mother's face closer to her child's—reveals Mantegna's proximity to Donatello's Madonnas. Donatello's holy mother holds her baby as tightly in a bronze relief in the church of Saint Anthony in Padua, and in his marble *Pazzi Madonna*, her face leans onto her baby's face.

The baby cries, perhaps in fear of being torn away from his mother, perhaps as he will later cry on the cross. His cloth covering is a compelling detail that likens the semi-transparent stripes of white linen wrapping the newborn like bandages to the canvas upon which it is painted. The canvas is exposed due to the paint scraping away, lending its woven grid to the texture of the shroud-like wrap. The marble window informs us of Christ's future grave.

Already one of the most famous artists in northern Italy and the favorite of the intellectual elite, Mantegna was about twenty-three years old when he painted *The Presentation of Christ in the Temple*. Not commissioned and in private possession, it was probably painted in celebration of his marriage to Nicolosia in 1453 and the birth of their first son the following year. Indeed, as much as this picture gives shape to the idea of sacrifice with splendor, it seems personal and intimate, a devotional painting that is also a family portrait. In the second row of Mantegna's painting, Joseph's head faces us as his gaze is directed at Simeon with awe and a slightly wrinkled forehead. Two haloless figures dressed in modern clothing can be seen on the painting's edges: a young woman on the left side, presumably Mantegna's young wife, and a young man at the far right, partly concealed by the marble frame. He is staring absently into the pictorial space. Since the early nineteenth century, it has been identified as a self-portrait of Mantegna himself.

Nicolosia was Giovanni Bellini's half-sister and daughter of Jacopo, the paterfamilias of Venice's most acclaimed family of artists. Jacopo might have wanted the young prodigy Mantegna to work for him in his workshop, while his son-in-law, the self-made carpenter's son, had other plans. Already as a seventeen-year-old prodigy and realizing his capacities, Mantegna went to court against his possessive teacher and adoptive father Francesco Squarcione (also a self-made man, less a painter than an entrepreneur with an eye for great talent; Squarcione founded the first private art academy in Italy in Padua) to liberate himself from his obligation to the elder man. In 1459, soon after his wedding, Mantegna would become the court painter, in fact the artistic director of the Gonzaga dukes in Mantua, and move there from Padua with his family. There he would live and work until the end of his life forty-seven years later. Besides painting over the course of almost half a century, he would dictate the taste and design of architecture, sculpture, jewelry, tapestry, and embroidery as well as theater settings for the Gonzagas.

Mantegna's unusual close-up grouping around the Madonna and Child in *The Presentation* has a dual effect. Likely derived from the principle of an icon as a work that is both intimate and deeply formal, it compresses the space as though seen through a long-focus lens: the scene is brought close to us in all its detail while remaining forever remote. The painted marble framing defines a barrier, indicating the "paintingness" of the protagonists within it, but also suggesting a latent trespassing into the viewer's world. This is most so with the infant, held on a cushion placed on the lower edge of the marble window. Mary's elbow on the frame, pointing toward the viewer, declares a trompe l'oeil that pulls us inside the frame as much as it pushes the painting's boundaries into reality, drawing us closer in an unprecedented way, yet keeping the happening remote.

An almost identical (at first sight, at least) twin painting of the *Presentation* hangs in Fondazione Querini Stampalia in Venice. For centuries, the origin of the two strikingly similar yet inherently different paintings has been disputed, but both were often credited to Mantegna. One enigma was solved, and another appeared, when it turned out that the Venice painting was made some twenty years later than the one in Berlin and that it had been created by Giovanni Bellini, Mantegna's Venetian contemporary and brother-in-law. It was additionally discovered that Bellini had not only been inspired by the Berlin painting but had traced Mantegna's work to transfer its contours. Bellini's painting was also not a commission, and probably made around the time of the death of his father, Jacopo.

The two paintings encapsulate the complex relationship between Mantegna and Bellini, which was also the subject of an erudite but spectacular exhibition in Berlin's Gemäldegalerie in spring 2019. There the two paintings were presented together next to each other for the first time. Bellini's *Presentation* exudes a warm tranquility. The colors are redder, and the artist elongated its composition and added two figures, one at each side. He removed the haloes and while in Mantegna's painting each hair is carefully rendered with the old technique of egg tempera on canvas, Bellini's picture has become altogether smoother, harmonious and less drastic than Mantegna's. Bellini painted with oil on a wood panel. He was one of the first to adopt the new oil technique soon to overtake most of European painting. It arrived in Venice from across the Alps through northern artists like Jan van Eyck, having elaborated painting with an unprecedented degree of detail, setting in motion its transformation to an artistic medium in its own right.

Not only did Bellini turn the marble frame to a parapet, nothing of Mantegna's sculptural thinking is left in his variation. The humanist poet and Venetian friend Ulisse degli Aleotti wrote that Mantegna "sculpted in paint." Aleotti praised Mantegna's lifelike painting, but this very quality was charged against the artist already in his lifetime by his abandoned Paduan teacher Squarcione and Giorgio Vasari, who in his biography accused him of making figures that look like stone statues rather than living flesh. Several centuries later, Bernard Berenson also claimed that Mantegna painted people "as if they were made of colored marble rather than of flesh and blood," imposing a bias against Mantegna among some influential twentieth-century art historians and critics as far as *The New Yorker*'s Peter Schjeldahl.

"Today, for all of us, Giovanni Bellini stands higher as an example of independence of spirit than Mantegna and, a fortiori, than every other Venetian or Paduan contemporary," wrote art historian Roberto Longhi in the early twentieth century. Longhi's lifelong desire was to reverse the commonly acknowledged indebtedness of Bellini to his older brother-in-law by claiming he was born ten years earlier. Mantegna's admiration of antiquity and humanism made him too much of a pagan, an "archaist" with too little religious sense (Berenson) or too much of a devotional Christian failing the sensuality of a real pagan (Gombrich). He was too arrogant, too "academic," too much of a technical virtuoso and too revealing of how he did what he did.

Could it be that the aforementioned critics have altogether missed—something strikingly evident in the 2019 exhibition—that Mantegna's thinking in sculptural terms does not diminish the intimate, thoughtful empathy he shows toward his protagonists? Did they not see that the specific human characteristics of Mantegna's protagonists have transformed them from iconographic figures to individuals? Dressed in contemporary clothing, their bodies carry physical weight. They are elevated and ideal, but also concrete; they are both sculpted and flesh. Standing in front of the painting, it is hard not to sense what the picture shows: a painter's emotional awe, affected equally by the threads of motherhood and the gospel, and by the immersion of these two traits with each other.

The pairing of the two *Presentations* demonstrated the intensity of the two painters' mutual influence and the striking differences between their approaches. The exhibition showed how the dichotomies by which the two were categorized and judged over the centuries in an eternal evaluation contest about who was the greater artist fail to meet the understanding of the sixty-year dialogue between them and what it meant to be an authoritative and inventive artist in the fifteenth century.

In 1504, a Venetian art dealer wrote to Isabella d'Este, wife of Francesco Gonzaga, herself a knowledgeable collector of antiques and patron of both artists: "Nobody can beat Mr. Andrea Mantegna for invention, in which he is the height of excellence ... but in color Giovanni Bellini is excellent." According to Giovanni Santi, Raphael's father and the court painter to Federico da Montefeltro, the Duke of Urbino, his patron was "was struck dumb" (*stupefatto*—stupefied or speechless) by Mantegna's pictures. His literal description implied not only Mantegna ranking above all other Italian painters including Piero della Francesca, but painting's triumph over words.

Comparing the artists' backgrounds—the privileged brilliant son as opposed to the self-made orphaned virtuoso, having had to fight his way up since the age of ten—it is easier to connect the free, harmonious, smooth sweetness radiating from almost any Bellini painting (the collection in Berlin is rich in paintings by Bellini) to a notion of an optimist Renaissance or at least the nineteenth-century idea of it. Known to be a slow-working perfectionist, Mantegna's understanding of human nature is perhaps a more pessimistic one, whose dark sharpness pushed him to uncompromising edges.

"All historians know," Kenneth Clark said in a lecture delivered to the Royal Society of Arts on Mantegna in 1958, that "our knowledge of the past is based almost entirely on the records of litigation; and for this reason, our knowledge of Mantegna at all periods is remarkably full." Roger Fry, too, described the artist in 1905 as "... quarrelsome, morose, litigious. We hear of him most as an ill neighbor, an unhappy father, an indiscreet and aged lover." It is therefore remarkable that this proud, ambitious, and difficult man "almost more of a humanist than an artist" (Fry) painted some of the most tender pictures of the Madonna and Child in Christian art. All facts notwithstanding: "All the penalty, all the humiliation of a 'made flesh' existence, his Madonna and Child present a mystery to us. They live a life whose feelings are unknown—intense but too restless to be divine," Fry wrote.[1] Mantegna's is a realism submitted to detail like the Flemish paintings that had surely influenced him, but still unexpectedly dark and mystical.

1 Roger Fry, "Mantegna as a Mystic," *The Burlington Magazine for Connoisseurs* (Vol. 8, No. 32, 1905); and "Madonna and Child by Andrea Mantegna," (Vol. 62, No. 359, February 1933).

Shadow of Existence

Self-Portrait I and *II* (1649 and 1650) by Nicolas Poussin

The moment Narcissus discovered his reflection in the water is recounted by Leon Battista Alberti as the origin of painting: the art of capturing the image seen on the uncertain surface. The Renaissance man complemented his trope with a different source, quoting Roman rhetorician Quintilian, who claimed that the earliest painters demarcated shadows made by the sun. Alberti, in his 1436 treatise *Della Pittura*, ignores at this point a more memorable story connected to this idea of origin that appears in Pliny's *Natural History*, a story of a Corinthian potter's daughter who invented drawing by tracing the outline of her absent lover's shadow on the wall with a piece of chalk.

Between capturing the specular image—"What is painting but the artful embracing of the surface?"Alberti rhetorically asks his friends—and enclosing the shadow as means of keeping the image of a lover in memory, painting is invented.

"I shall send you the one that comes out best," the painter Nicolas Poussin wrote in a letter on June 20, 1649, to his friend and somewhat envious client Paul Fréart de Chantelou. After acquiring some of Poussin's most accomplished paintings in the 1640s, de Chantelou had now requested a portrait of the artist. "But you must say nothing about it, please, to avoid causing any jealousy," Poussin continued, referring to another, similar commission he had been busy with from another patron, Jean Pointel.[1] Behind Poussin's cautious pledge was Chantelou's envy over the painting *Moses Found in the Waters of the Nile* (1638), which was made for Pointel.

1 See Louis Marin, *Sublime Poussin*, trans. Catherine Porter, (Palo Alto, 1999), pp. 183–208.

NICOLAVS POVSSINVS ANDELYENSIS ACADEMICVS ROMANVS
PICTOR ORDINARIVS LVDOVICI IVSTI REGIS GALLIÆ. ANNO
1649. Romæ.
ÆTATIS SVÆ. 55.

Everything connected to Poussin's two self-portraits is elusive and has been the subject of much speculation. They were the only self-portraits the French painter working in Rome ever created. Why did Poussin end up painting the works, when neither patron required it? Why did he make them so similar? Why did he not make them identical? He painted them at the height of his career, despite the genre's inferiority—his oeuvre includes only one other portrait, proof of his principal distaste or discomfort with this kind of undertaking. Yet apparently finding no suitable painter for the double commission ("There is now no one in Rome who does good portraits," he wrote to Chantelou), he decided to fulfill the task himself.

We more likely owe the making of this cryptic pair of paintings to the latent rivalry between the two collectors, Poussin's commitment to both, and his fear of disappointing the more emotional patron. "I am not like those people who, even though they are singing, always have the same tone; I know how to change when I want to," he wrote in a letter to Chantelou two years previously on March 24, 1647. Indeed, the twofold commission had led him to painting the two self-portraits almost at the same time. But these portraits—of the painter and, as is often the case, of painting itself—present a repetition rather than a copy; a doubling that emphasizes a difference precisely in its similarity. Poussin treats the "self-portrait" as a structure upon which he makes two variations.[2] As the subject of the painting, the painter must make himself an object. This split, whose integration is called *self-awareness*, inevitably defines any attempt to capture or grasp oneself. Poussin addresses this here, twice: he shows not only the self-portrait as something that is in its essence dual, split, and differentiated; but also painting—pictorial representation as such.

Despite the fact that the painter testified to have been making two self-portraits, for many years Pointel's painting, in the Berlin

2 Poussin describes the principle of variation in a letter to Chantelou, to teach him how to look at paintings. Marin compares the two portraits to musical variations making the painter a subject. Can the imitation of self by self be solved by the principle, the system of musical variation? "What Poussin is proposing is [...] two 'manners,' two variations of two modes of painting that are presented by the figure of the painter himself. The figure we call Poussin's self-portrait masks, or perhaps *is* a mask, for Poussin's theoretical propositions concerning manners of painting." ... "The painter repeats himself not in his identity but in his difference." Marin 1999 (see note 1).

collection since 1821, circulated with unclear status.[3] Was it a sketch? A study for the painting intended for Chantelou? Was it a copy made by Poussin, or by someone else? In 1953, the work was at last confidently identified as the original picture painted by Poussin in 1649 for Pointel: a copy of this painting in London was believed until then to be the original.

Pointel's *Self-Portrait I* shows Poussin in half-length in front of a trompe-l'oeil bas-relief on a stone plaque, a tomb. A laurel garland held by two cropped putti frames his slightly tilted head. The picture's space is flat and crowded. The painter's figure fills it, enclosed from the back by the tombstone and from above by an inscription of Poussin's biography (as a 1660 engraving of it testifies, a later owner mercilessly cut the work's upper edge). Yet it is open to the sides, with the little putti facing the space beyond the picture, offering communication with the world outside.

The script over the painter's head listing Poussin's name, origins, status, the current date, and his age is almost identical to an epitaph on a tomb of Poussin's friend, the Flemish sculptor François Duquesnoy in Rome. Poussin has positioned his painted head—the face and body more tender than in the later, denser *Self-Portrait II* at the Louvre Museum in Paris, which was sent as promised to Chantelou in spring 1650—in front of the tomb, where the portrait of the deceased would have been seen. The portrayal of the painter, however, seems rather alive. He turns halfway toward the viewer, his gaze directed beyond the picture to the observer or perhaps to his own reflection in a mirror.

It depicts a gesture of melancholy and the contemplative temperament that brought the painting into being. In place of the deceased, Poussin portrays himself twice, first with his written name and age (the epitaph on the tomb) and with his painted figure. Forever fifty-five years old, surrounded by laurels of glory held by baby putti, decorating the dead and celebrating birth, painting is marked as a place of decline and emergence.

3 Pointel's work was later part of the collection of Edward Solly, an English merchant living in Berlin (1776–1844). The painting was purchased by the Prussian state for the newly founded Alte Nationalgalerie (Old National Gallery).

Poussin detested Caravaggio and famously said of him that he came into the world "to destroy painting." Both of the contemporaneous painters (Poussin was a bit younger) addressed the crisis of representational art in the sixteenth century in Italy in ways that could not have been more different, yet both convey an enduring dichotomy in understanding and conceptualizing the pictorial space and painting. Overcoming the boxlike character of a picture now independent from architecture (in contrast to altarpieces or murals) in Caravaggio's paintings, figures confront the viewer openly for the first time. The viewer is entangled within the painting's sphere, experiencing its action. Poussin was suspicious of this notion. In Poussin's pictures, the figures appear absorbed and completely unaware of the viewer's existence; in fact, they wall off the observer from the drama taking place in what later will be defined as tableau paintings. Interestingly, each of these divergent approaches opened a path leading to modern painting, which crystalized in the twentieth century. "Read the story and the painting," Poussin wrote to Chantelou, when he gave him the painting *The Israelites Gathering the Manna* (1638) ten years earlier, indicating the way he understood his paintings were to be untangled.

Poussin's paintings are meant to apply a distance within themselves and in relation to the beholder. They are encoded with a secretive subtext in which biblical and mythological motifs want to be read allegorically. Seeking to revive Renaissance values of expression of feelings through gesture (*affetti*) and the relying of artistic representation on perspective as a geometric instrument, perhaps Poussin tried to protect himself against a certain "theatricalization" of art and the world emerging in Rome around 1630 with the rise of new kinds of viewers, to whose self-regard and confidence painting was forced to submit. The outcome was a distance intrinsic to his paintings, which likely preceded technological image-making in its essence, yet could never still be surpassed by it.

His hands crossed like wings of a bird in *Self-Portrait I* (the right covered by the left) suggest multiple dialectical inversions necessary for the painting to be made and perceived, according to Poussin. The inversion made by the mirror a reflecting mechanism essential for a self-portrait, the dialectic transposition between the figure and its ground, between the picture's inside and its outside and finally between the theory and the praxis of painting. The painter in this *Self-Portrait* is holding a drawing pen, indicating his profession, and a book titled *Light and Color*. The inscription, however, was apparently added after the painting left the artist's studio. Devoted restorers who discovered this in 1994 decided then to remove it, and with it any doubt in this regard. Either way, this book was never written by the artist, who has chosen to portray himself here with a book rather than a canvas and was known as an intellectual, writer, researcher, and a poet. And while the title points to light, shade, and color as elements of both vision and the painting, indicating Poussin's interest in color theory and the science of optics as well as in a rational judgment of painting, the title's vertical script, like the horizontal script above, also demonstrates (in and as painting) the competition between writing and painting in art's pursuit of defeating ephemerality. In this case, architecture—stone, tomb, monument—and sculpture belong to the art of the image. The pen is illuminated; the book dimmed by shadow.

This kind of concurrence between media was common in artworks of the era. Once, when asked by a stranger where he could buy good antiques in Rome, Poussin replied by picking up a handful of local Roman dust, offering it to the stranger and saying: "Let me give you the most beautiful antique you could ever desire," pointing to the transience of material works of art, painting, and sculpture alike.

If the two self-portraits were placed beside each other, it would seem that Poussin had straightened up his figure in the later portrait (1650), adopted a more severe expression, and pushed the space back to fill the painting with the painter's workshop, which replaces the tomb as a background. The black toga the painter wears in both portraits is indeed a hybrid between a Roman mourning dress and a workers' gown typical for seventeenth-century Rome. A series of overlapping right angles frames the face of the painter in his workshop. By equally revealing and concealing, the workshop backdrop analyzes the process of painting, in which every detail stands in for painting itself. Straight behind the painter, we see a canvas turned away from us. Behind this undisclosed painting, a canvas faces us, featuring a head of a three-eyed Hellenic woman, with the third eye decorating the crown on her head. She in turn is embraced in the arms of an incomplete figure outside the picture.

While in Pointel's self-portrait the putti reach their arms to the outside and beyond the picture, in Chantelou's the outside comes inside, reaching into the picture and into the painting. The edges of both self-portraits serve as an active threshold, a place of interchange between the inside and the outside of the painting. It is a limit that animates the allegory of painting as it defines its ends.

Finally, on the unpainted canvas facing the viewer is a golden script reading:

> Effigies Nicolai Poussini Andel:
> Yensis Pictoris. Anno aetatis 56
> Romae Anno Jubilei
> 1650.
>
> (Portrait of Nicolas Poussin of Andel-Ys, painter. In the year of his age 56 in Rome, the jubilee year 1650.)

The painter's own shadow darkens the script on the ready-to-be-painted gray canvas. The script is cropped by the painting's edge, like the figure on the opposite edge reaching her arms out from "off-stage" to embrace the Hellenic woman, or perhaps to pull her out of the painting. Both of the painting's sides indicate, in word and image, that what we see is always also what we do not see; what is visible within the frame belongs to or continues outside it. The signature's text separates the person from the painter, subject, and model, and clarifies the allegory of representation. "Effigies," the word Poussin added to Chantelou's picture signature, means indeed a portrait, a statue, an image; but also a shadow or a ghost.[4] Dropped upon the not yet painted canvas, the painter's shadow slips, too, outside of the painting's frame. It fills the unpainted canvas like a prophecy of the painting to be made, and a substitute, an inevitable ghostly companion to all living things depicted. The self-portrait *is* a shadow.

With these self-portraits, two almost identical paintings secretly painted at almost the same time, a series of duplications occurs:

the self, Poussin, his portrait (the alienation and fragmentation inherent to the act of seeing oneself wherein the self is being objectified, becoming an Other); and finally the painter's figure of himself and its shadow, which duplicates his being into a visible figure, and an invisible one. Something invisible (a ghost?) is made visible.

If friendship makes faraway people seem present, painting, Alberti wrote, has a divine power to set the deceased before our eyes. Those looking at the images of the dead enjoy the presence of the absent and admire the painter's skill at one and the same time. Is the power of painting more elevated than that of friendship? In his self-portraits, Poussin contemplates the question of portrait painting and ephemerality. Will the newly created presence make us forget the absence of the represented person, or will this presence remind us of the absence?

4 Man is said to have been created in God's image in the first chapter of Genesis: "In our image, after our likeness." The original Hebrew text reads צלם *tselem*: a shape, a figure, an image, a cast. Yet like the Latin "effigies," the word includes *tsel*, meaning darkness and shadow. Maybe from the ultimate beginning, the ur-moment of image-making, the creation of man (cast in the form of a formless God), shape is entangled with shadow.

Nature's Plan

Landscape with St. Matthew and the Angel (1640) by Nicolas Poussin

A curve in the river leads to a ruined city, depicted thoroughly and reductively in a near-geometric arrangement. The Torre delle Milizie—the fortified square tower from which persistent legend has it Nero observed the monumental fire devastating ancient Rome in AD 64—identifies the city. But although the massive tower in the painting *Landscape with St. Matthew and the Angel* (1640) recurs in several of Nicolas Poussin's landscapes, as does the Roman Campagna area, the sites' specificity seems secondary. It is as if the places and landmarks were elevated and their ideal essences extracted into elementary shapes: a cube, a cylinder, a sphere, or a cone.

Closer to the Tiber's curve, Matthew the Evangelist is sitting on a bankside stone, writing. An illuminated angel, his divine attribute, instructs the evangelist with a whisper, his finger pointing at the script, the first of the four Gospels. Symbiotically joined like a two-headed creature, they are surrounded by scattered architectural fragments, column drums, partial roofs, pillars, and an ashlar. Matthew and the angel are rooted in the sandy earth in light brown hues, as if they were growing from it. The light falls evenly; the scene is clear. The view is like a cinematic establishing shot, a sequence condensed to a singular picture to indicate to viewers far outside of and above it what will take place in a story that is suspended, forever unfolding in the distance.

Working in Rome for most of his life, Poussin's view developed in a society with a rising taste for the spectacular. In the mid-seventeenth century, the Counter-Reformation's energetic popes were quickly commissioning churches and newly cut thoroughfares, modifying the city with exuberant theatricality and art that was meant to overwhelm the senses. This was also the case with Lorenzo Bernini, who dominated the Roman art world of the seventeenth century, serving several popes and cardinals. A novel kind of art viewing emerged at the time in private art galleries, as did a new kind of art viewer who was a knowledgeable connoisseur, a dilettante at times, to whose self-regard and contentment painting tended to submit. Poussin's Classicism—his turn toward the pure origins of art of the past to study antique Greco-Roman sculptures and fragments and gradually to a Stoic restraint in order to revive art using bold colors and clear contours instead of freer brushwork—must therefore also be seen in this context. It was a measure of resistance to this kind of dramatization of art and the world that would soon be designated as the Baroque style.

Assimilated into the ruins, Matthew and the angel are completely isolated. There are no signs of life, only vestiges thereof: a white cloak is draped near the two fair, bare feet protruding from the evangelist's blue-orange gown and the angel's ivory dress as though they were one body. The cloak's folds in ivory white, reverberating the color of clouds above and of the angel's dress, imitate a dead body. A decapitated corpse. Is it pointing to Saint Matthew's end? According to tradition, he was stabbed—assassinated while saying Mass in Ethiopia, as unforgettably depicted in Caravaggio's painting *The Martyrdom of St. Matthew* at San Luigi dei Francesi (1599–1600). Either way, the architectural ruins in the painting serve as a visual metaphor of the debris left behind by history's vicissitudes. Like the writing of Matthew the historiographer, ruins remain to testify to the transience of life and things. Itself a fragment, Matthew's text is a memory of the fleeting moment of the angel's lost speech. And so writing is born, like this painting, from memory and speech; between the living Matthew and the figure of his death.

Poussin was inspired by or inevitably related to the philosophical works of contemporaries such as Roland Fréart de Chambray, who admired the artist and for whom geometry was the source and guide of all the arts; or René Descartes, for whom geometric order helped prove the existence of God; or, finally, Galileo Galilei, who wrote that philosophy could not be comprehended without knowledge of mathematical language and its characters: triangles, circles, and other geometric figures. Consequently, the appearance of things with Poussin is always complicit with their rational nature and organic order. Specific places in his landscapes are gradually permeated with a universal language in which each shape is always also its own paradigm.

Not that Poussin didn't study nature firsthand. Like many painters of the seventeenth century, plentiful drawings testify to his systematic studies and mastering of naturalistic representation. "I have seen him … study even stones, lumps of clay and sticks of wood in order to better represent rocks, terraced plots, and tree trunks," wrote André Félibien, a French diplomat, writer on art, and one of four biographers who met Poussin in Rome.[1] We also know that Poussin made excursions to the Agro Romano twenty years before making this painting. In his multivolume biography, German painter and theorist Joachim von Sandrart recounts how he accompanied Poussin in his first years in Rome into the surrounding countryside to draw from nature with a fellow younger French exile Claude Lorrain, whose dreamy golden pre-Romantic landscapes could not have been more different from Poussin's.[2] They rode on horseback along the Tiber just beyond the gates of Rome until Tivoli. It might have been after one such expedition that Poussin famously said, "I have left nothing unheeded."

Indeed, in *Landscape with St. Matthew*, Poussin does not seek to reflect a specific time, area, or vegetation. His studies are evidently accurate but used merely as a tool. This painting is considered the first of Poussin's classic or heroic landscapes, the kind of paintings that he gradually elaborated upon to become his quintessential artistic achievement of reviving or reinventing nature through its ideal. Poussin's vision of nature is embedded in his conception of art as intellectual in essence. His expeditions are journeys in search of an immanence, an "all is one and one is all."[3] Poussin approaches nature in search of a proposition of the whole, for which nature stands and

1 See Claude Lévi-Strauss, *Look, Listen, Read*, trans. Brian C. Singer (New York, 1997), p. 33.
2 Pierre Rosenberg and Keith Christiansen, eds., *Poussin and Nature: Arcadian Visions*, exh. cat. Metropolitan Museum of Art (New York, 2008), p. 46.
3 Later, in the nineteenth century, this would perhaps be called the Absolute in German idealism and, differently, by various Romantics. Here, the work of art has a special place as the only way to think of the whole, to activate the Absolute.

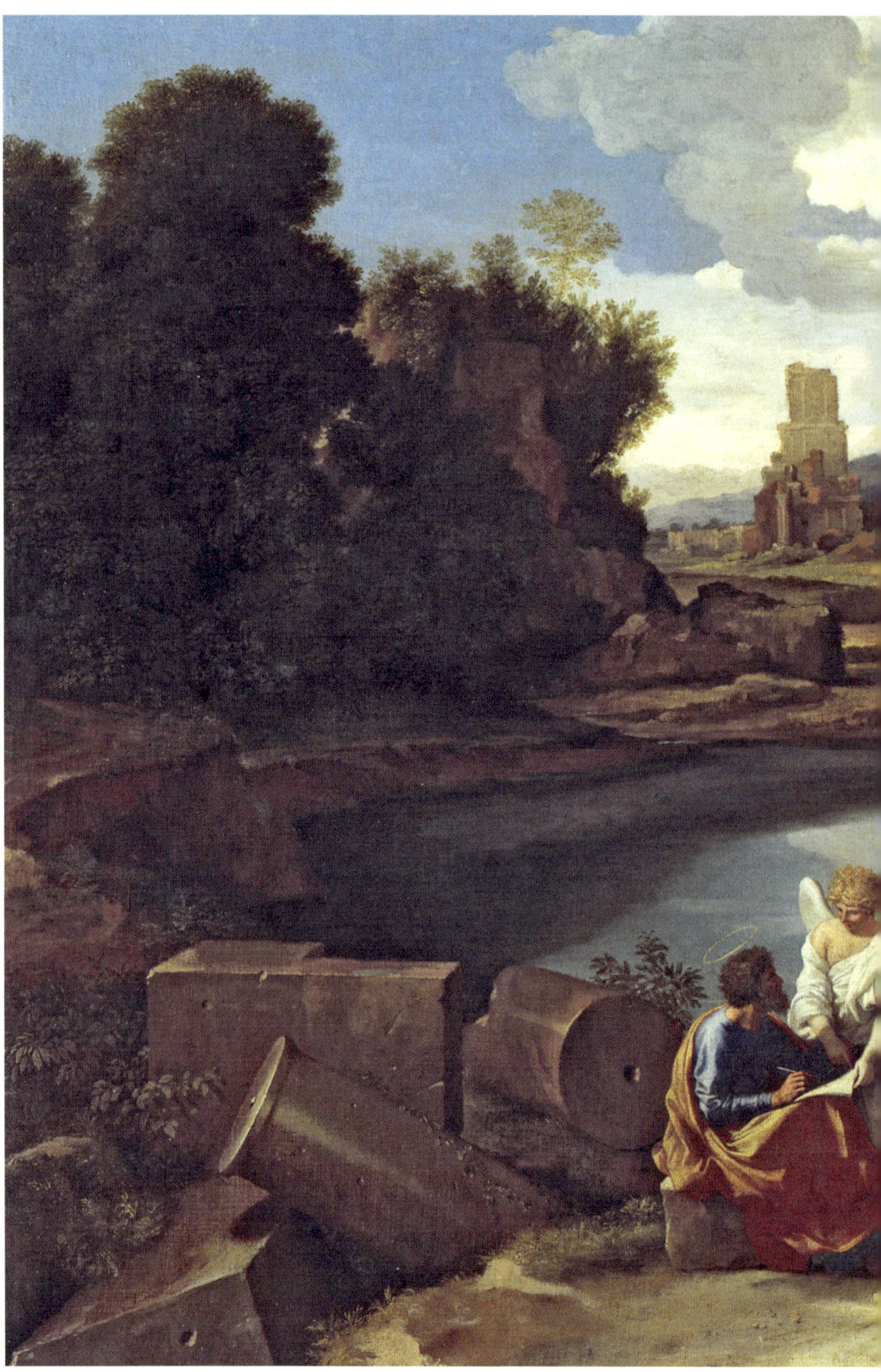

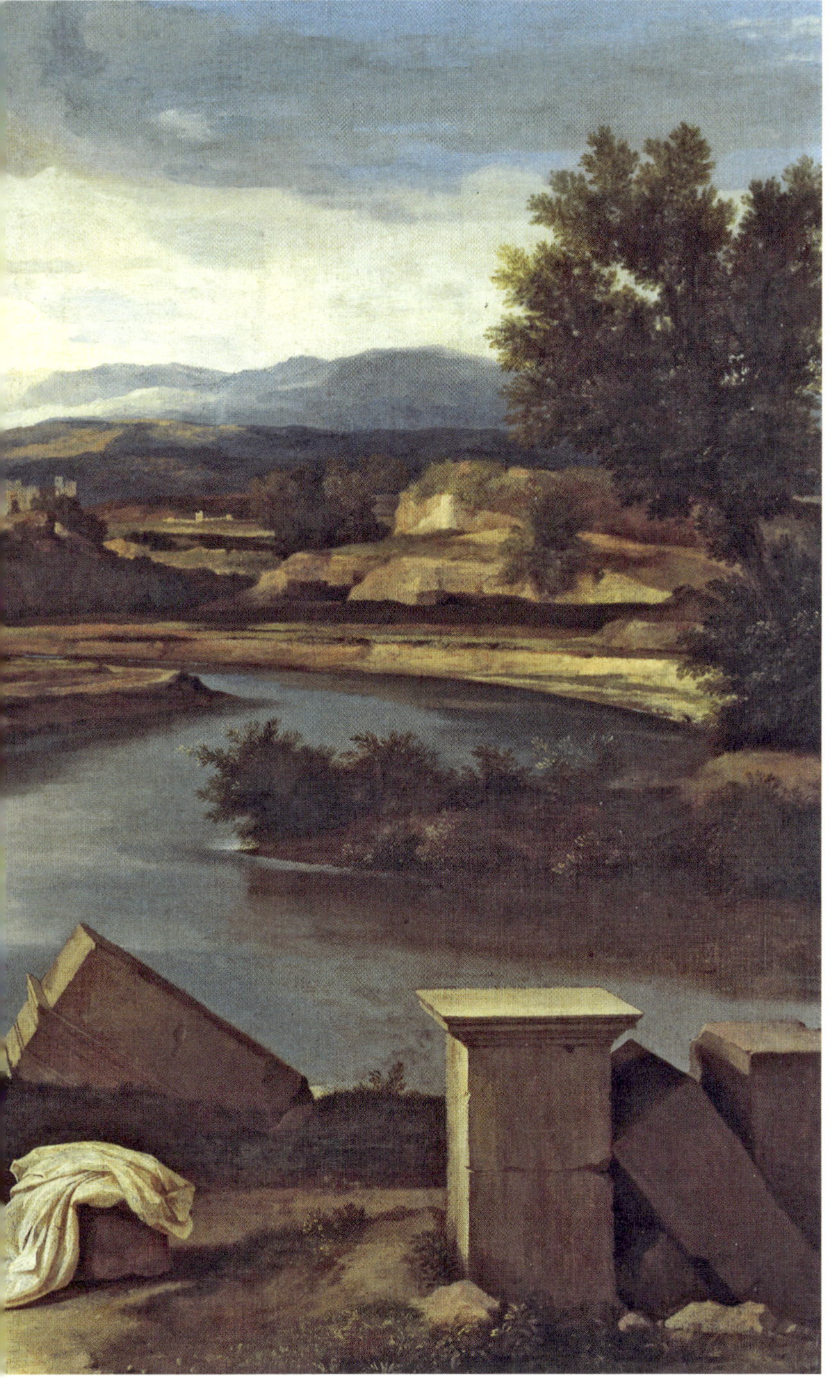

that nature is part of. A whole where there is a predetermined order that is beautiful and imbued with reason, like in the classical Greek cosmos.[4] Poussin's nature is a cosmic reproduction; an imitation of eternity where all things move toward the fulfillment of their potential, like a seed that becomes a tree. Out of the organic flow of nature, a geometric scheme prevails, underscoring harmony as the innate order of the world. His order is thus no longer completely a God (neither Hellenistic nor Christian, but is still far from being the mechanical, atomic early modern order of nature; the scientific revolution's nature in which nothing grows or yearns in this cosmic sense.

St. Matthew is likely part of a never-completed series on the four Evangelists. The painting has a counterpart, however, from the same year: *Landscape with Saint John on Patmos*, today in The Art Institute of Chicago. Since the death of their commissioner and first owner in 1644 only four years after their creation, the two paintings have rarely been united. Giovanni Maria Roscioli, secretary to Pope Urban VIII and a noted art collector, paid Poussin forty écus for both paintings in October 1640.

John the Evangelist is portrayed writing while he is banished on the Greek island of Patmos, a juxtaposition to the apocalyptic, violent visions of The Book of Revelations he is working on. The eagle in profile, his attribute, standing for the Revelations' surreal vision of the first man as half eagle, retreats from John with his back to him, unlike Matthew's angel, who is harmoniously united with him—and with the rigorous order of the surrounding nature. On *Landscape with Saint John on Patmos*, the eye runs obliquely through a series of zigzags, curves, and barricades from the ruins in the foreground, then through a thicket of trees to a middle ground along the hillside, and finally to the meandering river in the background.

Like Matthew, John is surrounded by architectural fragments, "as if the place for sacred writing, for the poem of revelation, could be only a field of ruins," philosopher and scholar Louis Marin suggests.[5] The Christian sacred writing on the end of time, with its violent, surreal visions, takes place in a landscape testifying to the

4 Nature is the order where all beings: plants, animals, and man alike, act and move.
5 Louis Marin, *Sublime Poussin*, trans. Catherine Porter (Palo Alto, 1999), p. 149.

passage of time, a collage of ruins (like the city of Rome itself) made of layered histories and destructions and collapsed civilizations: the Egyptian obelisk, a Corinthian temple, landmarks of ancient Rome such as Hadrian's tomb in the distant background. It is as though Saint John's body echoes a triangle that is also formed by the ruins in the right foreground, repeated at the top of the obelisk, displaying an utterly geometric construction of the world: nature's very architecture and man's humble place within it. But while, in *Saint John*, temples and obelisks rise behind a curtain of trees to a populated seaside town with homes and palaces, in *St. Matthew* the river leads to a ruined city.

The two paintings from 1640 mark a moment in which the conception of nature in painting changes for Poussin, and is gradually transformed from being merely a setting, a coulisse of sorts, into a protagonist in its own right: a pictorial element equal in status to other figures inhabiting it. Here, nature is no longer described but rather *re-formed*. The landscape we see is still. The water in the river in *St. Matthew* does not flow; no wind blows in the trees. What distinguishes the water from the stone? The polished columns from the figures of the Evangelist and the angel? Man and object, nature and architecture blend and invert. The river is almost solid, the architectural ruins grow organically from the earth, animating the painting's foreground.

Like nature, the figures in the painting seem more sculpted than painted on canvas. The painting is like a mosaic in which each piece retains its own face and character, Claude Lévi-Strauss wrote.[6] Denis Diderot called Poussin's figures "naïve," that is, "being most perfectly and purely what they must be." To create his works, Poussin used an optical box with landscape backgrounds, arranged as required in order to utilize the specific landscape for the sake of a greater, universal purpose. Before undertaking a new painting, Poussin would shape small wax figures, pose them on boards within the boxes, and drape them in cloth, molding the folds with a stick. Through holes in the boxes, he could design the light falling on the figures and measure the shadows' positions. The presence of the three-dimensional

6 Lévi-Strauss 1997 (see note 1).

model is clearly visible in this painting. The model conveys a dominance of the world over individuals that are tranquil sculptures in a serene setting: timeless, ideal, eternal.

Paul Cézanne, some two hundred years later and at first sight a complete antithesis to Poussin in almost every respect, notably discussed "doing Poussin on nature." With Cézanne, too, nature seems extracted or converted to its rudimentary essence. Could it be that both painters, fathers of modern French painting, arrived at such geometry—an almost Cubist abstraction of nature—from opposite directions? Poussin's abstraction was grounded in Classicism and idealism; Cézanne's emerged from sensation and his devotion to what he saw, to what one sees. Both seem to have transfigured imitation in favor of something else. Distant from each other in their mimetic gestures—Cézanne's with an expressive attempt to approach nature from the surface and Poussin's by means of an ideal construction—each takes a first step toward abstraction, or at least reveals how much the figurative is always involved with the abstracted. In different manners and with divergent motives, each painter separates representation from description.

Landscape with Satyr Family (1507) by Albrecht Altdorfer

Three of Albrecht Altdorfer's earliest paintings from 1507 hang in a row in Berlin, close to Albrecht Dürer and Lucas Cranach the Elder—two of Altdorfer's most prominent older companions working, like him, north of the Alps. All seven paintings in the room by this artist, born around 1480, are relatively small and were most likely made for domestic spaces—succeeding the ancient icon, the portable painted panel was a most popular format for private devotional images in the sixteenth century. It became a useful format with which artists could both experiment and establish themselves. The smallest of Altdorfer's Gemäldegalerie paintings, *Landscape with Satyr Family*, is a bewildering panel about the size of an A4 sheet of paper, hardly larger than a miniature.

Under a dense thicket of trees, alongside a cliff, a group of three takes shelter: a furry horned satyr and his naked human bride with a child. With a spiteful look, the satyr reaches for a club. He is about to attack and prepares for a confrontation. Holding the child, his companion restrains him. Their gestures are strangely mirrored in a couple whose presence in a clearing in the background is not entirely explicable, but is evidently an unwelcome intrusion to the satyr family: a naked man with a stick holds onto a woman in a red dress and escorts her forceful stride into the forest.

The inscription on Altdorfer's tombstone in Regensburg describes him as a *Baumeister* (builder) rather than a painter. It remains unclear what role the eccentric oil paintings, watercolors, and etchings in his early career (all of which he signed and dated) played later in his life, but it is they, not his architectural achievements, that gained him his subsequent reputation. He died wealthy and successful in 1538 as a well-known municipal architect and political figure in the city.

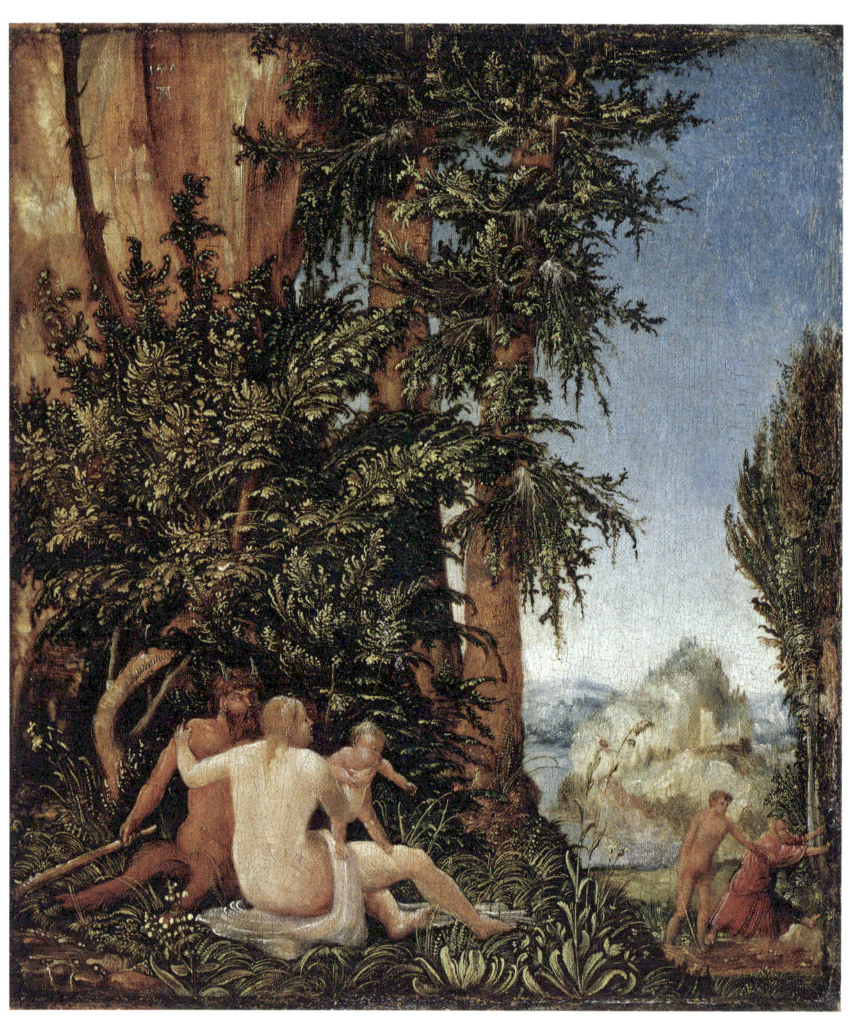

He owned three houses and presumably also planned and oversaw their construction. These stand in Regensburg until today.

An unresolved tension hovers over the scene in the painting. Multiple oppositions reflect each other in odd symmetry: the sheltered and the exposed; culture (the dressed woman, the distant castle or lodge) and nature. Does the couple in the distance represent a past moment in the satyr family? Do they pose a threat to free existence in harmony with wilderness? The painting's narrative plot is ambiguous, and its coarse setting lends the picture a strangeness. Two-thirds of the picture plane is filled with landscape, framing a slice of blue sky that creates a sense of depth in the work. A dark foliage in which all kinds of green leaves are highlighted with white lines covers thick brown tree trunks and a sandy ground in a tonality so rough it surrounds the protagonists with tangible wilderness. A smeared murky mountain in gray tones rises in the distance.

When nineteenth-century art historian G. F. Waagen, director of the Gemäldegalerie in Berlin from 1830 until 1864, saw the painting in Regensburg—with its towering thicket of trees and ornamental flora claiming so much of the canvas—he took it as an indication for how early the painter cultivated landscape as a genre in its own right, making the forest his true subject, rather than the featured figures. The narrative, he wrote in *Kunstwerke und Künstler in Deutschland*,[1] is merely a "staffage" which is "tasteless in invention as it is weak in drawing."

Against the tendency of northern artists who, especially after Jan van Eyck (1390–1441) were engaged in the enterprise of mirroring nature, copying it in utmost detail—Dürer's studies being a paragon—this early picture in Altdorfer's artistic career shows a different approach toward nature. Much more than imitation and a mere mimetic undertaking, the leaves, trees, and rocks in this picture seem to extend beyond its framing, and continue in their nearly inorganic overall repetition. They are made in a gesture that could almost be called expressive, an outcome of imagination. Nature becomes terrain for subjective projection. In *Satyr Family*, the explicit attention to vegetation and setting and the presentation of landscape deviates

1 See Gustav Friedrich Waagen, *Künstler und Kunstwerke in Deutschland* (Leipzig, 1843).

from the painting's small support. Consistent with its devotional format, this miniature panorama is more introspective than descriptive. A hallucination, it locates us in our own subjectivity.

The unforeseen appearance of landscape paintings and etchings in the Danube region—emerging from the margins or lower strips of prayer books, illuminated manuscripts, and miniatures—is sudden and unexplained. It occurred at about the time as the Italian Renaissance (Leonardo de Vinci would live twelve more years after the date on this small painting's signature) and in light of its important inventions, such as scientific perspective, anatomic knowledge and the rendering of the beautiful human body, and the rediscovery of classical architecture. In a 1966 essay on landscape painting in the Renaissance, art historian and author Ernst Gombrich suggested a solution to the mystery, pointing to the southern market's demand for such paintings, "a gift presented by the Renaissance South to the Gothic North." He cites a 1548 letter by painter Giorgio Vasari that read, "there is not a cobbler's house without a German landscape." But what seems to be the essay's most illuminating insight is the author's conclusion that sixteenth-century landscapes are not "views," but largely accumulations of individual features. They are conceptual rather than visual.[2] The illustration assigned to this point in Gombrich's piece is an etching made by Albrecht Altdorfer, dominated by a trunk of a pine tree, showing a mountainous landscape and a small town in fine lines.

And indeed, following the *Satyr* painting, Altdorfer eventually painted the first independent landscapes in European art history. These pictures are devoid of human or animal figures; they tell no stories. They feature a certain incompleteness and silence, three hundred years before the German Romantics elevated landscape painting—most distinctively with Casper David Friedrich—into a paradigm of the modern work of art. For Friedrich Schiller, a landscape painting or poem was to convert inanimate nature into a symbol of human nature. Nature appears in these paintings as something neither completely subjective nor objective but rather both a

2 Ernst Gombrich, "The Renaissance Theory of Art and Rise of Landscape," in *Norm and Form* (London, 1966), p. 116.

physical place and a personal experience. A memory of something we never saw or arrived at late, an image we discover while already knowing it. A fragment wrested from a whole that is allover and endless. An altar with no God.

Altdorfer was one of the first painters to make subject matter dispensable, and to place the formal over semantic-content completeness. He seems to literally bring the forest into the picture. Its thick layers of color, density, and compressed, closed space transcend an experience of being confined in the woods. Here, the forest is something bigger. Already in Altdorfer's lifetime most of the primeval forest was dissected by cities and roads. More an idea than a place, the German forest looms like a dark spring at the heart of what can be called German native fantasy. The forest became an emblem for the era's humanists; most influential was Conrad Celtis, whose educational vocation it was to turn the forest from the curse it seemed to incarnate—Roman historian Publius Cornelius Tacitus writes in *Germania*, an ethnographic study of Germanic tribes that Celtis republished in 1500, "a formless terrain and harsh climate, dismal to till or to behold unless it were one's native land"[3]—into a source of pride, originating Teutonic strength.[4] The forest was metamorphosed by the northern humanists to become an open-air temple, a home for muses, yet also harboring the frightening and barbaric satyr and the wild man.

Fantastical satyrs do not appear often in early German art. In Altdorfer's painting, the novel mythological figure of the satyr is fused with the northern European topos of the wild man. The hirsute, club-carrying, desirous wild man is one of German folk culture's specters, evoking imaginations and horror. In a Dürer engraving from 1505, a satyr blows a horn at his perhaps abducted female companion and her child. The horn is shaped as an extension of his erect penis. Altdorfer had probably seen a decorative tapestry featuring scenes from the life of the wild men from around 1400 hanging

3 See Larry Silver, "Forest Primeval, Albrecht Altdorfer and the German Wilderness Landscape" *Netherlands Quarterly for the History of Art* (Vol. 13, No. 1, 1983); see also Christopher S. Wood, *Albrecht Altdorfer and the Origins of Landscape* (Chicago, 1993).
4 Tacitus was the only ancient Roman writer on German antiquity that German humanists could rely on as positive source. He describes the ancient Germans as indigenous people.

in Regensburg's city hall. But unlike the doll-like depictions of forest life there, the wilderness in his *Satyr Family* determines its inhabitants, and not the other way around. This bestial creature of raw sexuality and militant spirit is antisocial through and through, an uncontrollable id force countering everything considered civilized.

In the sixteenth century, the satirical poet Hans Sachs from Nuremberg used the wild man who retires to the forest as his mouthpiece in speaking against civilization's wrongdoings. His poem "Klag der wilden Holzleut über die ungetrewe Welt" ("Lament of the Wild Man about the Unfaithful World") was decorated in 1504 with a woodcut by Hans Schäuffelein, which was, in turn, made after Dürer's engraving of *Adam and Eve* (1504), drawing the retreat to the wild as a return to the primeval innocence of the first man. Sachs's poem, after displaying a vivid catalog of society's corruptions, reads: "And so we left our worldly goods / To make our home in these deep woods / With our little ones protected / From the falsehood we rejected / We feed ourselves on native fruits / And from the earth dig tender roots / For drink pure springs are plentiful / For garments grass and leaves we take / And from the same our beds we make."[5] The freedom of life in the forest is not only brought as a fundamental innocence in contrast to the corruption of city life, but with Sachs, it also becomes a model of true anti-institutional *völkisch* version of piety and Christian humility. Altdorfer's diptych (1507) hanging beside the *Satyr Family* in Berlin and featuring hermit saints Jerome and Francis of Assisi in the forest, also demonstrates this notion of Christian wilderness, in which the forest almost obscures the figures.

Three centuries later, Sachs would be prominently featured in Richard Wagner's 1869 opera *Die Meistersinger von Nürnberg*. In a folk song competition at the center of the opera, Sachs is confronted with Sixtus Beckmesser, whose figure embodies a failed attempt at penetrating the circuit of German culture, which seeks to constitute itself first through the spirit (the song) and then corporally through his wishful coupling with a German maiden promised to the winning

5 Fred A. Childs and Timothy Husband, *The Wild Man: Medieval Myth and Symbolism*, exh. cat. The Metropolitan Museum of Art (New York, 1980), Appendix B.

singer. Sachs appears in the opera as as an archetype of German nativeness, and his folk songs serve Wagner's concept of art as a vehicle for social regeneration. Although Wagner did not explicitly define it as such, the figure of Beckmesser is permeated with anti-Semitic stereotypes. And indeed it came to be the infamous of Wagner's operas, due to its later key use in Nazi propaganda. Beckmesser's figure combines Wagner's arguments regarding the Jew as an alien agent that claims to embody the German spirit, but is in fact nothing but a "repugnant caricature of it."

The affinity to the uncivilized was an inseparable part of the search for a German past, in times of political and cultural assertion toward unity of the nation in the fifteenth and sixteenth centuries. Celtis, one of the humanists around the Holy Roman Emperor Maximilian I, had ties to scientists and literates in Regensburg. It is not unlikely that Altdorfer was aware of his writings. Either way, the search for a German antiquity meant, for the northern humanists, an attempt to concur with the glory of the classical one. It gradually evolved into hostility toward Italian culture as part of a certain popular patriotism. This conjoined to an idealization of all that was unknown to civilization described as wild or primitive—in this contest between the North and the South, barbarism was always mirrored in primitivist appreciation and archaism—at the time when the first explorers to the New World began to return to Europe with their troves.

Could it be that remnants of a longing for the subversive, for sheer wilderness (even if castrated, modified, or reconceptualized), can be found in postwar German painting through the twentieth century, perhaps even until today?[6] It certainly had informed the figure of the rebellious artist—a Nietzschean outsider or criminal outcast—as a wild man, and the wild man as an artist. It cannot be considered without what began to take shape in Altdorfer's *Satyr Family*.

6 With the sterile exception of Gerhard Richter, all postwar German painters from Georg Baselitz and Eugen Schönebeck through Anselm Kiefer, Jörg Immendorf, Sigmar Polke, Blinky Palermo, Albert and Markus Oehlen, and finally Martin Kippenberger—all share in their personae and art an affinity to the masculine, bohemian, wild, drunk, clownish artist figure. Joseph Beuys before them represents his own, not unrelated, category.

The True Image

The Holy Face of Christ–Vera Icon (ca. 1420) by an unknown Westphalian artist

Mysterious imprints of Jesus Christ's face have turned up in Christian traditions since the sixth century. These portraits are said to have been created when a piece of fabric was pressed against Christ's holy face or body. The exceptional images, altogether five or six, are considered acheiropoietic—that is, not made by a human hand, but rather through a miracle: the miracle of the Vera Icon (True Image.)

Such was the *Holy Towel of Edessa (Mandylion)*, which appeared in Constantinople in 944. Known to have protected the Mesopotamian city of Edessa under several sieges, it was taken as booty by the Byzantine Emperor Romanos I after he defeated the Muslim rule of the city. The *Mandylion* was welcomed with a grand ceremony and then copied and disseminated as a popular icon through Byzantine art. Legend has it that the towel originated in Mesopotamia with Abgar, the king of Edessa and contemporary of Jesus. He was allegedly cured of leprosy by the acheiropoietic portrait of Christ impressed on a cloth, brought to him by a direct disciple of the son of God. The towel disappeared, reappeared in France, and was finally lost, most appropriately, during the French Revolution. A replica on two cypress panels, considered true to the original *Mandylion*, was sent in 1249 from Rome to a convent near Laon, a city in northern France. From there it was moved to the Laon Cathedral in the eighteenth century, where it can be revered today.

The Laon Face's journey from the east may have predated the Western *Veil of Veronica*, also called *Sudarium*. This cloth fragment carrying an imprint of the Holy Face is still praised alongside the wood of the cross in Saint Peter's Basilica. Only in the fourteenth century did Veronica become prominent in the Western church, tying together different threads of True Images. The myth of a compassionate

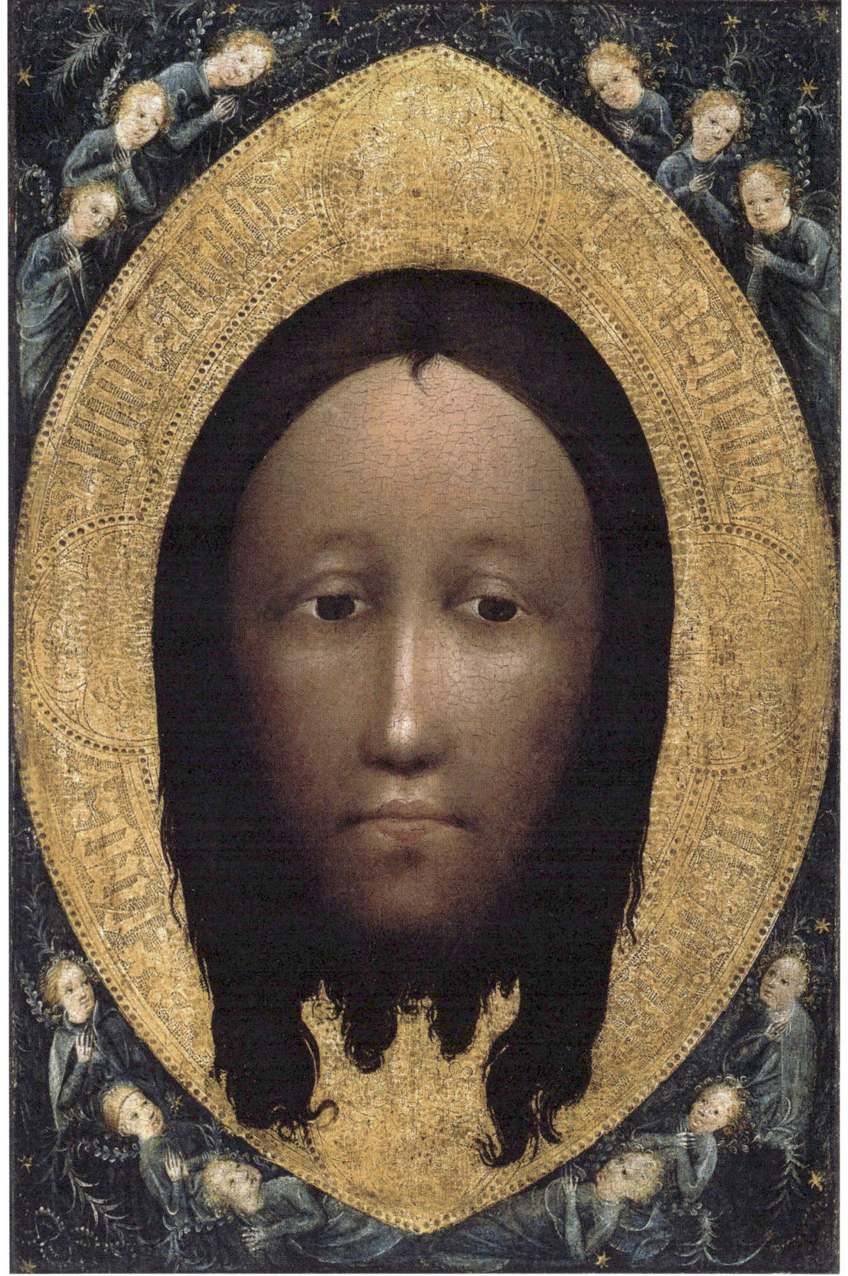

woman who watched Jesus carrying the heavy cross on his back and then wiped the sweat from his head to see that his face was marked on the cloth was linked to Veronica (in Latin, Berenika), the woman who suffered from twelve years of continual menstrual bleeding until she touched the fringes of Jesus's cloak. In another legend, she intended to paint his portrait, but rather received a miraculous copy of it from him on a veil. In an etymological twist, Veronica was finally interpreted as comprising the words "Vera Icon."

Both relic and photograph, the veil predicts the mechanical image, or rather haunts it, as a prospect of a picture that is not handmade but an outcome of contact; an image that is a souvenir or trace of an event.[1] Notably, these fabric relics, assuming to bear witness to incarnation, don't show much when they are seen. What is visible is a faint figure, smeared or completely effaced, mostly revealing the objects' material—a wrinkled piece of textile, a handkerchief—a canvas of sorts.

Medieval images of the Holy Face therefore have a peculiar status. They are considered "true," but behave as though they were merely replicas (or replicas of *the* replica). They exist in the ritual domain as icons and are pivotal as paintings. By declaring these images true and divinely made, a human desire is at work to eliminate that fact that representation is always (also) a concealment and bring forth an image that will *show* and not *obscure*, an image that is not a representation but rather makes the Holy Word present once and for all. The connection to reality that they seek, as all images do, conveys a human wish to connect or declare loyalty to another world.

In the Westphalian *Vera Icon* in the Gemäldegalerie, painted on an oak panel, the disembodied head of Christ floats freely over a

1 Roland Barthes asserted that photographs are acheiropoietic in *Camera Lucida* (New York, 1981), p. 82. The image upon the Shroud of Turin, according to legend Jesus's burial shroud and one of the famed acheiropoietic relics today, can apparently only be seen in a negative photograph. This was first observed by a photographer pilgrim in 1898, only three decades after the photographic inventions of Louis Daguerre and Henry Fox Talbot, when "spiritual photography" bloomed. It was believed to prove the survival of the soul after death by capturing it in a photograph. Since its invention, photography was associated with life after death, since it provided a mechanical impression of reality for the first time in human history.

golden mandorla, an almond-shaped framing typical for medieval icons. Emerging from a dark ring of beard and hair is a face with deep brown eyes; turned inward and yet directed at those who look at him. Simple *sfumato* is enough to animate the face, making it expressively human compared to the common graphic rendering of icons, and raising it from the flat ornamented surface like a magical revelation.

Many features in this Holy Face correspond to a description of Jesus found in the apocryphal Letter of Lentulus, a report on Jesus allegedly written by Publius Lentulus, a Roman procurator of Judea, to the Roman Senate. "His hair is of the color of the ripe hazelnut, straight down to the ears, but below the ears wavy and curled, with a bluish and bright reflection, flowing over his shoulders. It is parted in two on the top of the head, after the pattern of the Nazarenes. His beard is abundant, of the color of his hair, not long, but divided at the chin."[2] Many German and Netherlandish paintings from the fourteenth century onward coincide with this Lentulus description, although historians have not confirmed the existence of such a Roman procurator and the text was dated no earlier than the thirteenth century.

Whether the fabricated text verified the paintings or vice versa, this standardized depiction of the Holy Face corroborates the purpose it was devoted to fulfill: to translate an invisible world to a visible one. Like a dream seen only retroactively through its verbal description, both image and text point to, and attempt to compensate for, a missing prototype. In the Westphalian icon, as was often the case, a text is also integrated into the picture as a remnant from the other representational system of incarnation: the Word, the original vehicle of creation as we know it and as it was first transmitted. In the golden mandorla surrounding the visage from left to right like a halo, an inscription reveals the words of the redeemer, and refer to the first and last letters of the Greek alphabet, that is, to language as means of creation: *Ego sum alpha et o (mega) deus et homo*. I am Alpha and Omega, the beginning and the end, God and man.

The Holy Face is repeatedly enclosed; framed by the dark curly hair and beard, the inscription, the golden mandorla, the panel's

2 Montague Rhodes James, *The Apocryphal New Testament* (London, 1975) pp. 477–78.

edges where three individually featured angels bow from within each of the work's four corners and finally, an additional frame painted in blood red and decorated with medallions, each encircling a flower. Could it be that the blood of Veronica, as well as Jesus's marks of blood and sweat on the cloth, lingered on the red frame of the Westphalian panel? Does this blood connect the Passion of Christ with the decapitated head?

There is no literal justification for such a staging—a disembodied, androgyne, Gorgon-like head hovering over the flat surface—yet it is featured in many versions of the Holy Face,[3] such as the Laon Face. Something of the magical, talismanic qualities attributed to relics have survived in the icon's frame, making it an active site of meaning. While picture frames from the Renaissance until the modern avant-garde surround what they depict like a window through which a piece of the world is viewed, supporting its mimetic nature and presuming a single subjective viewpoint (cognition), the icon's frame defines and classifies a world completely separated from reality.

Purchased in 1842–3 by the Gemäldegalerie from a collection in the city of Soest in Westphalia for 113 Reichstaler and ten Silbergroschen, this Holy Face is one of the only icon painting panels in central Europe that has remained intact. Even the forged steel hooks on its back are probably original. They indicate that it hung in private homes as an object of veneration. A reduction of time spent in purgatory was granted to those reciting the prayer *Salve sancta facies nostri redemptoris* (Hail, O Holy Face of our Redeemer)[4]—which promises admission to heaven at the end of time—in front of a True Image with Christ's face. The more the value of the indulgence increased over time, from ten days in the thirteenth century to ten thousand in the late fifteenth century, the more the popularity of the Veronica cult rose.

3 That the Holy Face recalls the head of Medusa (two instances too terrible and mighty to look at) suggests it integrated and appeased Greek and Christian pictorial worlds; pagan talismanic qualities (the relics served as apotropaic weapons and allegedly protected the place where they were housed) with monotheistic beliefs. This suggestion appears independently in both Julia Kristeva, *The Severed Head* (New York, 2012), p. 6, and Georges Didi-Huberman, *Confronting Images*, trans. John Goodman (University Park, 2005).

4 Attributed to Pope John XXII and widespread prayer in the fourteenth century.

Thus, the meaning of indulgence underwent vast erosion, as did the idea of penitence abused by the political power of the church. A chasm was manifested in this process that is as old as the cult dance around the golden calf in the Bible concerning the nature of God's appearance and its image. The fissure between a desire to see God and the commandment prohibiting the worship of idols or images ("Thou shalt not make unto thee any graven image") have shaped each of the three monotheistic religions, as it did the evolution of Western image making as we know it. The Veronica cult was thus likely one of the symptomatic occurrences preparing the ground for the Reformation some one hundred years later; its iconoclasm undoubtedly echoed in the fierce quarrel between iconoclasts and iconophiles in the Byzantine church. This dispute took place about two centuries before the *Mandylion* arrived in Constantinople, yet it, too, evolved around the worship of an image of Christ. There is indeed no image of God, and perhaps no image at all, without this fracture. Not only the discrepancy between the word of God and "pagan travesty" or idolatry but also between the image's inherent attributes either as a presence or as an absence in the world.

When Kazimir Malevich unveiled the *Black Square* in an exhibition he called *The Last Exhibition of Futurist Painting 0.10*, in Petrograd (Saint Petersburg) in December 1915, introducing his Suprematist system to the world, he placed the piece high on the wall across the corner of the room, in the same sacred spot that an Orthodox icon would be placed in traditional Russian homes. "I've painted a naked icon of my time," he wrote in 1918 in a letter to his friend, the publisher Alexandre Benois. The eighty-centimeter black square on white canvas that he claimed was "the zero of form" was to be a defining moment for modern art. It was revealed to the world after months of secrecy and was hidden again for almost half a century after its creator's death.

Malevich (1879–1935) adamantly rejected all referents in the visual language of his paintings, emphasizing instead the painting's material qualities: texture, color, and spatial illusionism "as such."[5] But at the same time, Malevich called his pictorial system

5 See Masha Chelnova in "Abstraction 1910–1925, Eight Statements," *October*, Winter 2013 (143), pp. 3–51.

"new painterly realism," arguing that his aim was not to eschew the world of objects but to get closer to the true nature of reality. He gave many of his purely geometrical Suprematist compositions overtly referential titles, such as *Two dimensional painterly masses in a state of movement or Painterly realism of the footballer – painterly masses in two dimensions*, both from 1915.

With modern art, at least since Édouard Manet, "connection with reality" was once again separated from likeness, perhaps the illusions painting learned to create no longer provided the conviction in reality it was so obsessed in reflecting (with this withdrawing from resemblance, it has been claimed, painting made way for photography to be invented.)[6] With Malevich, painting was brought back to the question of how it can show something without depicting it. It is this question that challenges the simple binary distinction of figuration and abstraction and that seems to bond Malevich's *Black Square* with the icons of the Holy Face.

Icon (from the Greek *eikon*) means image, resemblance. Likeness seems to presuppose a referent, that is, that an image as such is an outcome that necessitates imitation, mimesis.[7] Against the urge plastic arts seem to have been driven by—to "embalm the dead" leading to a fixation on likeness, resolved or at least metamorphosed perhaps only with the invention of photography—the icon does not copy an object from the external world. It has no referent, at least not in reality, and it does not imitate. Rather, it wants to inscribe the presence of a religious experience. It wants to make us see God. It doesn't care about its singular beholder, who is in any case not a "viewer." In fact, less than seeing the True Image, beholders find themselves submitted to the image's gaze.

7 Discussing the ontology of the photographic image, André Bazin remarked that in the origin of painting and sculpture there lies a "mummy complex." *What is Cinema* (Berkeley, 1971), p. 195.

List of Illustrations

Cover; Flap, middle, backcover, and frontispiece: Historical views from the Gemäldegalerie and Skulpturensammlung in the Kaiser-Friedrich-Museum, Italian Paintings and Sculptures of the 15th and 16th century

Twelve primary paintings

Amor Vincit Omnia
(Love Triumphant),1601-02
Caravaggio (named), Michelangelo Merisi (1571–1610)
Canvas, 156.5 × 113.3 cm
Cat. Nr. 369
Acquired in 1815 from the collection of the Italian noble family Giustiniani
photo: Jörg P. Anders

Susanna and the Elders, 1647
Rembrandt Harmensz van Rijn (1606–1669)
Tropical wood (amaranth), 76.7 × 92.9 cm
Cat. Nr. 828E
Acquired in 1883 from Sir Edmund Lechmere, Worcestershire
photo: Christoph Schmidt

Joseph Accused by Potiphar's Wife, 1655
Rembrandt Harmensz van Rijn (1606–1669)
Canvas, 113.5 × 90 cm
Cat. Nr. 828H
Acquired in 1883 from Sir John Neeld (Grittleton House, Wiltshire) through the art dealer Charles Sedelmeyer, Paris
photo: Christoph Schmidt

Woman with a Pearl Necklace, 1663–65
Jan Vermeer (1632–1675)
Canvas, 56.1 × 47.4 cm
Cat. Nr. 912B
Acquired in 1874 with the B. Suermondt Collection
photo: Christoph Schmidt

Prince Heinrich Lubomirski as the Genius of Fame, 1787–88
Élisabeth Vigée-Lebrun (1755–1842)
Oak, 106.7 × 83.1 cm
Cat. Nr. 74.4
Acquired in 1874 from the Gallery Fr. Heim, Paris
photo: Jörg P. Anders

Étienne Chevalier with St. Stephen, ca. 1455
Jean Fouquet (1420–1481),
Oak, 95.9 × 88.2 cm
Cat. Nr. 1617
Acquired in 1889 from the Estate of the Brentano family
photo: Christoph Schmidt

The Madonna in the Church, ca. 1440
Jan van Eyck (1390/1400–1441),
Oak, 31.1 × 13.9 cm, semicircular at the top
Cat. Nr. 525C
Acquired in 1874 with the B. Suermondt Collection
photo: Jörg P. Anders

The Presentation of Christ in the Temple, ca. 1454
Andrea Mantegna (1431–1506)
Canvas, 77.1 × 94.4 cm
Cat. Nr. 29
Acquired in 1821 with the
Edward Solly Collection, Berlin
photo: Christoph Schmidt

Self-Portrait, 1649
Nicolas Poussin, (1594–1665)
Canvas, 78.7 × 64.8 cm
Cat. Nr. 1488
Acquired in 1821 with the
Edward Solly Collection, Berlin
photo: Jörg P. Anders

Landscape with St. Matthew and the Angel, 1640
Nicolas Poussin (1594–1665)
Canvas, 100.3 × 135.3 cm
Cat. Nr. 478 A
Acquired from the Palazzo Sciarra
in Rome in 1873
photo: Jörg P. Anders

Landscape with Satyr Family, 1507
Albrecht Altdorfer (ca. 1480–1538)
Lime wood, 23.1 × 20.4 cm
Cat. Nr. 638A
Acquired in 1874 with the
B. Suermondt Collection
photo: Jörg P. Anders

The Holy Face of Christ–Vera Icon, ca. 1420
Unknown Westphalian artist
Oak, 45.2 × 31.8 cm with frame
Cat. Nr. 1217
Acquired in 1843 from the collection of
District Court Council Dreckmann, Soest
photo: Jörg P. Anders

Additional paintings

Madonna Surrounded by Seraphim and Cherubim, ca. 1455
Jean Fouquet (1420–1481)
Oak, 94.2 x 85.3 cm
Inv. 132 Royal Museum of Antwerp
©artinflanders.be
photo: Dominique Provost

Self-Portrait, 1650
Nicolas Poussin (1594–1665)
Canvas, 98 × 74 cm
Inv. 7302 Musée du Louvre, Paris
© bpk | RMN - Grand Palais
photo: Jean-Gilles Berizzi

Tal Sterngast would like to thank Markus Farr, Stephan Kemperdick, Katja Kleinert, Sarah Salomon, and Sigrid Wollmeiner from the Gemäldegalerie and from the General Director's team at the Staatliche Museen zu Berlin as well as the staff at *Die Tageszeitung*, for their support. She extends her gratitude to Lena Kiessler from Hatje Cantz for her commitment and engagement, and to Sandra Bartoli, Ory Dessau, Ronald Düker, Philipp Graf, Drew Hammond, Dani Issler, Marianna Lieder, Silvan Linden, and Stefanie Peter for their attention and generosity.

Colophon

Managing editor
Lena Kiessler

Project management
Richard Viktor Hagemann

Copyediting
Kimberly Bradley

Translation into German and Copyediting
Ulrich Gutmair

Graphic design
Neil Holt

Cover design
studio stg

Typeface
Arnhem

Lithography and Production
Vinzenz Geppert

Printing and binding
GRASPO CZ, A.S.

www.smb.museum

Published by
Hatje Cantz Verlag GmbH
Mommsenstraße 27
10629 Berlin
www.hatjecantz.de
A Ganske Publishing Group Company

ISBN 978-3-7757-4767-7 (Print)

ISBN 978-3-7757-4801-8 (eBook)

Printed in the Czech Republic

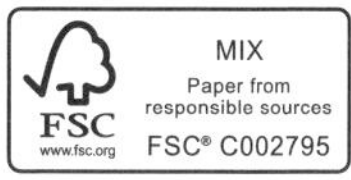